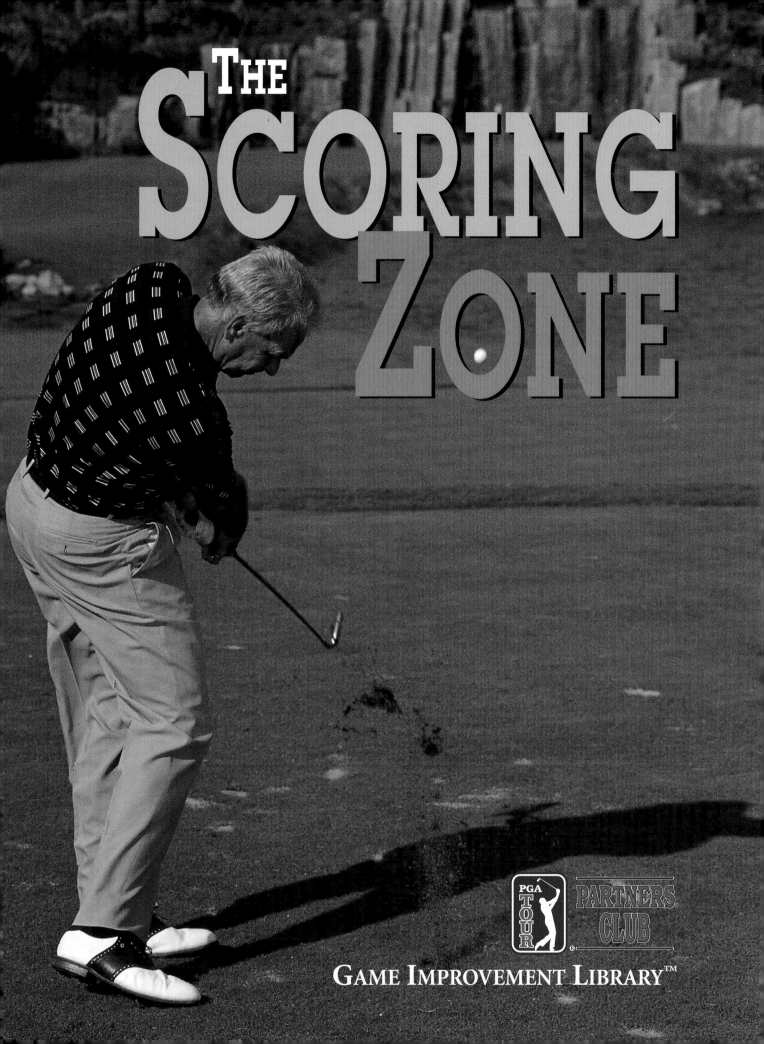

THE SCORING ZONE

PGA TOUR PARTNERS CLUB

GAME IMPROVEMENT LIBRARY™

CREDITS

THE SCORING ZONE

Mike Vail
Vice President, Product and Business Development

Tom Carpenter
Director of Book Development

Dan Kennedy
Book Production Manager

Julie Cisler
Book Design & Production

Jen Guinea
Book Development Coordinator

Steve Hosid
Instruction Editor/Photographer

Steve Ellis
Editor

Ward Clayton
Leo McCullagh
John Morris
Mike Mueller
PGA TOUR

Bruce Holt
Proofreader

Special thanks to the following golf courses for allowing us to shoot on location:
Trump International: Palm Beach, Florida
TPC of Scottsdale: Scottsdale, Arizona
TPC at Sawgrass: Ponte Vedra, Florida
DC Ranch: Scottsdale, Arizona
Ballen Isles: Palm Beach Gardens, Florida
Arnold Palmer's Bay Hill Club and Lodge:
   Orlando, Florida

Acknowledgements
"To the members of the PGA TOUR Partners Club I meet at Tournaments around the country: Your questions, comments and support help create articles and books that truly reflect the needs of our outstanding membership."
—Steve Hosid

8 7 6 5 4 3 2 1 / 07 06 05 04 03 02 01 00
ISBN 1-58159-119-5

PGA TOUR Partners Club
12301 Whitewater Drive
Minnetonka, Minnesota 55343

ABOUT THE AUTHOR/ PHOTOGRAPHER

Steve Hosid is instruction editor, contributing writer and photographer for *PGA TOUR Partners* magazine and for the Club's Game Improvement Library. He is coauthor of *The Complete Idiot's Guide to Healthy Stretching* (with Chris Verna), and *Golf for Everybody* (with Brad Brewer, former director of The Arnold Palmer Golf Academies), and has collaborated on books with LPGA star Michelle McGann and tennis player MaliVai Washington.

Steve is a graduate of the University of Southern California and has produced and hosted several television and radio shows in Los Angeles. These days his appearances revolve around golf on the PGA TOUR.

He lives with his wife, Jill, and two non-golfing Borzoi Wolfhounds on the 13th hole at Arnold Palmer's Bay Hill Club in Orlando, Florida.

Author/photographer Steve Hosid practicing his scoring zone game.

TABLE OF CONTENTS

Introduction

My friend David Leadbetter recently built a new practice facility called Champions Gate outside Orlando. This meticulously thought-out, world-class center is pure Leadbetter: innovative, comprehensive and reflective of his students' needs.

Imagine being able to re-create and practice virtually any scoring zone shot a golfer might encounter during a round. David did. Just as he revolutionized golf instruction for professionals and amateurs, Champions Gate sets the benchmark for practice centers.

I mention this because this book, *The Scoring Zone*, deals with an area of the game that offers the quickest and most logical way to lower scores. You may never be the longest off the tee, but that's just one stroke. The bottom line is how many more strokes it takes to get the ball in the hole.

In this book we present a slightly different view on how to approach the game. For most members the scoring zone starts 150 yards out and extends to the green, an area that theoretically should require a maximum of three additional strokes.

Our four PGA TOUR professionals prefer playing their highest percentage shot into the green from this distance, instead of reacting to where a drive or second shot landed, as amateurs tend to do.

We selected two dramatic holes to illustrate scoring zone strategy. Both are located on the Stadium Course at the Tournament Players Club at Sawgrass, site of THE PLAYERS Championship. The holes are the par 5 16th and the treacherous par 3 17th, the famous—or infamous—island hole.

Once inside the scoring zone, controlling accuracy and distance become the prime considerations, and we work diligently to help you improve.

After demonstrating pitching and chipping fundamentals,

our TOUR players will take you out on the course to face real situations. Join Bruce Fleisher as he punches his ball from under a tree. Stand near Billy Mayfair as he hits a high, soft lob over a bunker to a close pin. Tom Lehman will show you how to launch the ball high in the air from a steep downhill lie. And Mark McCumber provides valuable scoring zone strategy tips. That's just a sampling of what's ahead.

The Scoring Zone goes inside the minds of our pros as they work through their strategy and club selection, teaching you how to avoid stroke-costing mistakes.

But learning technique is only one aspect of game improvement. Renowned teacher Martin Hall's outstanding drills are the other key to a better game. You'll find Martin in the "Practice Tee" sections located throughout the book. *The Scoring Zone* even provides additional practice tips, as well as target drills that are both fun and time-efficient.

No matter who you are, how often you play golf or what your handicap, saving strokes is the name of the game. It's that simple. But there's also a simple plan for saving those strokes, a place where you can be most efficient at it. You've made your drive and we're walking down the fairway towards that critical place, the scoring zone. Let's begin.

-Steve Hosid-

Club President Tom Lehman holds up the ropes, inviting us to join him and the other pros out on the course—for detailed lessons and stroke-saving insights that will help you play better whenever you're in the scoring zone.

MEET THE PLAYERS

TOM LEHMAN

Born: March 7, 1959

Height: 6'2"

Weight: 190

College: University of Minnesota

1996 British Open Champion and PGA TOUR Player of the Year, winner of the Vardon Trophy and Nicklaus, Palmer and Nelson Awards. 1999 Ryder Cup Team. PGA TOUR Partners Club President.

BRUCE FLEISHER

Born: October 16, 1948

Height: 6'3"

Weight: 205

College: Miami-Dade Junior College

1999 SENIOR PGA TOUR Player of the Year. 1999 Byron Nelson Award winner for lowest scoring average and ranked No. 1 in birdie average per round. 1968 U.S. Amateur Champion.

Seventy percent of your score is derived from shots within 100 yards of the pin. With such a scoring impact, it pays to be at your very best within this distance.

As a kid growing up in Minnesota I realized the importance of having a good scoring zone game. My friends and I would play 18 or 36 holes, and by 6 p.m. there was still three hours of daylight left, so we practiced our putting and short game until dark or the mosquitoes drove us home. As kids we played games that taught us techniques I still use today.

For example, there was a 9-foot high sign next to the practice green that read "Welcome to Alexandria Golf Club." We would get behind that sign, maybe 10 feet away, and hit lob shots over it to the green to see who could get closest to the pin. Then we would see how close we could get to the sign and still hit a ball over it. When I got to within 3 feet of the sign, I learned to open the clubface wide and swing as hard as I could to hit the ball straight up into the air and land it just over the sign. So be inventive as you practice your scoring zone game.

—*Tom Lehman*

On the SENIOR TOUR fans often ask what was the secret to my success that made such a difference in my career. The answer is my scoring zone game. As the magic age of 50 grew closer, I made the decision to concentrate my efforts on improving my wedge play, chipping and putting.

Perhaps, like you, I had been spending too much time practicing the longer aspects of the game, like driving. It's a trap we all fall into. Now I only want to drive the ball into the fairway. Hitting my scoring clubs from the short grass gives me the best chance to make birdies.

It has been said many times that most people practice the part of their game that accounts for 80 percent of their strokes only 20 percent of the time. In pro-ams I see my amateur partners take two shots to go 400 yards, and then four more to get the ball into the hole. It doesn't take a Harvard education to figure out what part of their game needs to be improved the most. When I practice, I hit my wedges constantly and the other clubs only briefly, to work on timing and tempo.

—*Bruce Fleisher*

BILLY MAYFAIR

Born: August 6, 1966

Height: 5'8"

Weight: 175

College: Arizona State

Five-time winner on the PGA TOUR. 1995 TOUR Championship winner. 1986 U.S. Public Links champion. 1987 U.S. Amateur champion.

MARK McCUMBER

Born: September 7, 1951

Height: 5'8"

Weight: 170

10-time PGA TOUR winner. Won 1988 PLAYERS Championship and 1994 TOUR Championship. Golf course designer with his company, McCumber Golf.

Having an excellent scoring zone game on the PGA TOUR is imperative if you want to stay competitive, especially on days when you're not playing your best. On a par 5, for example, you can chip in for eagle and turn the day around.

The ability to get your ball close from just about anywhere helps you make the cut, stay in the tournament and have a chance for some outstanding rounds on the weekend. All golfers have a day when their long irons are missing greens and putts don't drop. Let your short game rescue you.

The way I hit a shot is different than how most other pros might hit the same shot. In fact, for every shot there may be four or five different ways to execute it. The key is to choose the method that feels the most comfortable for you, and that you're confident in, for the situation.

I love to practice. It's part of my work ethic. On TOUR, the emphasis shifts to playing. But when I'm home, I practice a lot because I enjoy it, especially my short game. That's the time to use your imagination and experiment, even while working on the basics. When I play, every shot I hit from 150 yards and in, I feel I can make.

—Billy Mayfair

You can't play golf without a positive attitude. The closer you get to the hole, the more positive you must become. Targets become smaller and are surrounded by hazards. Tension increases.

Remember the great times you had as a kid trying new things, being inventive, and enjoying the thrill of actually pulling off some impossible shot? Play with the same attitude you had then, and enjoy the challenge.

When I was growing up in Florida we moved to a house on a dirt road. It was across the street from a Donald Ross-designed public golf course, so that was the first front yard I remember. My brothers and I used a set of my mom's clubs and we would hit balls to the trees in our backyard. It wasn't until I was 7 years old that I actually got to play on a real golf course.

—Mark McCumber

MARTIN HALL

Martin Hall, one of the game's top instructors, provides his proven practice drills throughout this book. Hall appears regularly on the PGA TOUR Partners Video Series and has been selected as one of the 50 best golf instructors in the U.S.

1 HOW GOOD ARE YOU IN THE SCORING ZONE?

The flag flutters temptingly from 150 yards and in, inviting you to hit the ball close. Even missing the green isn't disastrous here, if you know how to execute the next shot to get close enough to one-putt.

Do you presently have the knowledge and shot-making skills to consistently score well once you're inside the "Scoring Zone"?

Perhaps the best way to find out is by having our four PGA TOUR professionals and fellow PGA TOUR Partners Club members—Tom Lehman, Bruce Fleisher, Billy Mayfair and Mark McCumber—answer a few of your questions on their scoring zone games.

How do TOUR players make the ball spin when it lands on the green? Why do their shots fly high and land softly, instead of soaring out of sight, when they take a full swing close to the green? How do they consistently pitch and run the ball close to the hole?

Before they reveal their secrets and transform you into a scoring zone star, here's our chance to ask a few questions about the critical scoring zone game.

PRO: TOM LEHMAN

QUESTION: WHAT PERCENTAGE OF GREENS SHOULD I BE HITTING IN REGULATION?

ANSWER:

A green in regulation (GIR) refers to the number of greens you hit in a round that leave you with a birdie putt. For example, on a par 4 you would have reached the green in regulation if your second shot landed on the green. On the PGA TOUR, a 64-percent GIR is average, and the statistical leader typically is in the low 70s. If you reach 80 percent of the greens in regulation, have you considered going to one of the TOUR's qualifying schools?

On a par 4, chances are your scoring zone shot is from between 80 to 150 yards out, depending upon whether you are playing your second, third or fourth shot. The key from this distance is accuracy. The only way to be accurate is to master the basic fundamentals—grip, alignment and posture. Bruce Fleisher and Martin Hall offer help in Chapter 3. Martin makes sure your swing plane is up to par on pages 62-65. **— TL**

PRO: BILLY MAYFAIR

QUESTION: HOW IMPORTANT IS KNOWING THE DISTANCE I CAN HIT MY SCORING ZONE CLUBS?

ANSWER:

Golf is my job and clubs are the tools of my trade. At this level of golf, I better choose the correct club for the job at hand. I know the distance I can hit every club in my bag, so once I know the distance to a specific target or pin, choosing the correct club is easy.

Knowing the distance to the target is an important first step toward proper club selection. I'll help you with determining distance and show you how to evaluate the distance for each club on page 29. Once you have this knowledge, it will instill in you the confidence you need to commit to the shot. You will feel more confident once you know which club in your bag will deliver your ball a specific distance to the target. **— BM**

PRO: BRUCE FLEISHER

QUESTION: HOW CAN I IMPROVE MY WEDGE PLAY?

ANSWER:

I attribute my good fortune on the SENIOR PGA TOUR to improving both my wedge game and my putting. Ideally, every wedge you hit should leave you close enough for a one-putt. The key is to know which wedges to carry in your bag and how to hit them properly.

Most TOUR players carry three wedges, which underscores the importance we attach to this phase of the game. We'll show you our wedge choices on page 70. You can learn more about wedge technology on pages 155-156. If your friend's luck around the greens has changed for the better recently, you may want to take a look in his or her bag too.

Having the best equipment is one thing, but I had to re-learn my game to benefit from it. I'll show you my approach to wedge play in Chapter 5. Martin Hall offers some outstanding drills beginning on page 83.   **— BF**

PRO: MARK McCUMBER

QUESTION: WHAT'S THE DIFFERENCE BETWEEN PITCHING AND CHIPPING?

ANSWER:

A pitch shot brings the ball onto the green along a higher trajectory and from a longer distance than a chip shot. A chip shot is hit from just off the green and stays close to the ground before landing and rolling to the pin.

You can also play a pitch-and-run, landing the ball off the green and allowing it to scrub off some speed before rolling onto the green. When you end up short of the green, it's valuable to know how to play several different shots, rather than always playing the same type of shot with limited success.

Throughout the book we will show you how we decide which way to play a shot. We will also challenge you to make the decision first before we reveal our preference.   **— MM**

PRO: TOM LEHMAN

QUESTION: WHAT ARE THE KEYS TO A GOOD PITCHING GAME?

ANSWER:

Pitching the ball close to the pin can rescue a potentially bad hole. It also offers an alternative to lobbing the ball high into the air, and may be an easier shot for most members to hit consistently.

Hitting a pitching wedge does not mean you hit a pitch shot. Pitching wedges can send the ball high and land it softly on the green. In this instance, the height of the trajectory will not allow much roll after the ball lands.

With a pitch shot, the ball comes in higher than a chip shot, but it will release and roll after landing. Distance control is crucial.

You can learn more about controlling distance in Chapter 6. Martin Hall demonstrates drills on pages 99-105. **— TL**

PRO: BILLY MAYFAIR

QUESTION: HOW IMPORTANT IS THE CHIPPING GAME?

ANSWER:

Once I get into the scoring zone, I feel that I can hole any shot. This is especially true when chipping. When I pull the trigger, I expect the ball to go into the hole. I don't sink them all, but all golfers should make some. The real key is mastering the proper technique. Think of how many strokes you can save.

In Chapter 7, we show you how to chip close to the hole consistently. There is strategy involved with technique. Martin Hall demonstrates the putting chip on page 124. His chipping drills, beginning on page 125, will also help. **— BM**

PRO: BRUCE FLEISHER

QUESTION: CAN I ADJUST MY SCORING ZONE GAME DEPENDING ON THE BALL'S LIE?

ANSWER:

When the ball is below your feet, you have to play the shot differently than when the ball is level or above your feet. Any difference in terrain requires some adjustment, or disaster will result.

In Chapter 5, Tom Lehman demonstrates how he plays uphill and downhill shots, and how he plays a ball above or below his feet. I have some suggestions for what to do on uphill or downhill chip shots in Chapter 7.

We can show you what to do, but you have to practice to develop the feeling necessary to hit these shots consistently. When Tom Watson made his dramatic chip-in from a difficult lie to win the 1982 U.S. Open at Pebble Beach, he attributed his success to practicing that shot. **— BF**

PRO: MARK McCUMBER

QUESTION: WHAT ARE THE KEYS TO A GOOD SAND GAME FROM THE BUNKERS?

ANSWER:

Bunker play is not that difficult. In some situations, professionals actually aim for bunkers during a tournament because it may be easier to spin the ball out of the bunker than off the ground.

Of course, none of that helps if your stomach churns whenever you see sand on the horizon. While it would take another book to teach you all you need to know about making sand your friend, we demonstrate some sand basics in Chapter 8. Bruce Fleisher will show you how to execute shots from fairway bunkers on page 58. **— MM**

Pro: Tom Lehman

Question: How Can I Spin a Ball on the Green?

Answer:

Lee Trevino once answered the question about spin by asking why an amateur would want to spin the ball back when they are short of the pin most of the time. Hopefully, after testing to see how far you hit each club, landing short will be a thing of the past.

All balls spin, but when they stop and jump back after hitting the green, that is a combination of the club, ball and ground coming together, plus above-average hand\eye coordination and loads of practice. Getting a ball to spin backward like that requires a tight fairway that doesn't allow grass to get between the ball and clubface, as well as a high-spin ball with a soft feel and cover.

Billy Mayfair demonstrates the spin shot on page 142. There are other ways you can hit the ball past the pin and have it come back. You will learn how professionals use the green's topography and aim to targets that offer a "backboard effect" in Chapter 2. On page 105, Martin Hall demonstrates drills to help you slide your wedge under the ball, causing enough spin to stop it once it lands.

— TL

Pro: Billy Mayfair

Question: How Inventive Should I Get with My Scoring Zone Game?

Answer:

This is one of my favorite subjects. The short game is comprised of feel and imagination. My suggestion is to begin on the practice range, away from the pressures of your round.

Using the fundamentals and techniques in this book as a starting point, try several different adaptations of those shots and compare the results. Switch clubs and try the same adaptations. Be creative and inventive to see what happens. Vary the length of your swing, the ball position and the degrees you open your clubface.

I practice some of these shots in Chapter 6. When TV announcers comment about a player's inventiveness, I guarantee we have hit that same shot thousands of times before, while practicing.

— BM

PRO: BRUCE FLEISHER

QUESTION: HOW CAN I HIT A BETTER SHOT OFF HARDPAN, PINE NEEDLES OR FROM BEHIND A TREE?

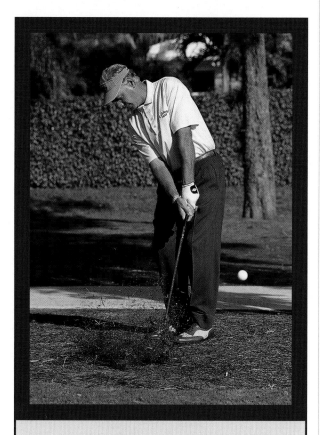

ANSWER:

Shots like those tax even a TOUR player's ability. But there is a way to play every shot, regardless of what you face, although the quality of the outcome may vary.

On pages 130-131, I demonstrate how to hit off a surface that is extremely hard. The key is the club used, ball position and making an arm swing with a descending blow.

Pine needles or soft, unpredictable lies are also dealt with in Chapter 8. You often see pros facing similar shots at the Masters. Rescuing yourself when a tree gets in the way is demonstrated in the same chapter.

— BF

PRO: MARK McCUMBER

QUESTION: DO I NEED TO PRACTICE MY SCORING ZONE GAME?

ANSWER:

Success comes from practice. At the professional level, the best players constantly work hard, just as any successful individual prepares to reach the highest levels of his or her profession. When we are at tournament sites, fans have a good view of the driving range but they seldom see us practice our short game.

Everyone can find an hour at least once a week to practice. In Chapter 9, Partners Club member Andy Warden demonstrates some practice drills we suggest you try.

Martin Hall's "Practice Tee" drills also can be done in your backyard or in a park. If you want to become a better player, there are no excuses for not practicing. The fast track to success is improving the quality of your scoring zone game.

— MM

2

SCORING ZONE STRATEGY

Executing the perfect shot every time you arrive in the "Scoring Zone" is secondary to understanding the strategy in becoming a better player. Before showing you how to hit specific shots, (the subject of future chapters), our professionals will provide strategy tips to help you develop a more proficient scoring zone mentality.

Mark McCumber, who won THE PLAYERS Championship in 1988, begins by sharing his strategic decisions on two holes on the Stadium Course at the Tournament Players Club at Sawgrass, site of THE PLAYERS; these holes seem to always impact the outcome of the tournament. And Mark explains why the scoring zone really begins on the tee.

You will be able to incorporate the players' strategies immediately into your game. For instance, did you know that an approach shot checks up faster if the grain on the green is growing toward you?

Billy Mayfair teaches you how to find the distance you hit each club. This is invaluable if you want to become a consistently good scoring zone player. After reading this chapter, you will be able to pick the correct club to hit the shots described.

So please turn the page and join Mark McCumber on the 16th hole at TPC Sawgrass.

THE SCORING ZONE BEGINS ON THE TEE!

Start your scoring zone improvement by thinking differently about how a hole should be played. Instead of mentally playing a hole from tee to green, reverse the order and play from the green back to the tee.

On the PGA TOUR, we want to play the highest percentage shot to the green. Pin placement sheets provide exact pin locations, and yardage books reveal topography and other relevant information. Armed with these guides, a TOUR professional decides the type of shot and the distance he wants to play it from, for the crucial scoring zone approach.

Mark McCumber.

Most players prefer a yardage that allows a full shot into the green. He may choose a long iron or 3-wood off the tee to get to that spot, instead of a driver. This is especially true on par 5s. We will lay up on our second shot if the percentages are not in our favor to go for the green in two.

The par 5 16th hole at TPC Sawgrass is a good example.

WHAT SCORING ZONE SHOT WOULD YOU PLAY?

From the tee on this 497-yard, dogleg left hole, the green (inset photo) is hidden by the trees. Water runs down the right side from tee to green, and you can see a line of trees guarding the left. A back left pin with a green guarded by large trees whose branches extend over the fairway are part of this beautifully designed hole.

Would your name be on the list of those who automatically would hit a driver off the tee? If your philosophy is to hit it long and then hit it long again on par 5s, please accept my condolences. You just made my casualty list. You just fell for a sucker setup, and your third shot to the green would likely be blocked by those trees guarding the green.

With this pin placement, I would never go for the green in two. My scoring zone strategy would be to choose the best spot to play a full-swing approach shot. How to best reach that spot with my second shot is key to what club I select to hit off the tee.

START WITH PIN PLACEMENT

Most amateurs never consider pin placement. This pin is located 17 yards back on a green that slopes from back to front. Behind me you can see a ridge that runs from the front of the green to the back. Landing right of the ridge moves the ball away from the hole, while landing past the hole leaves a difficult downhill putt. The approach shot should be played as if there is no green to the right and no green past the hole.

This is one time when ending up 10 feet away may not be as good as 20 feet if you are on the wrong side of the hole. Uphill putts are easier than downhill putts, so the ideal shot would be short and on the left side of the green. Even if you come up short of the green, you're left with an easy chip up the slope.

This is the sucker part of the hole. Hitting a driver off the tee and a fairway wood for the second shot could bring an average golfer to this yardage and this headache. The fairway sharply narrows, and trouble lurks above.

The high trees eliminate a lofted shot, while the water behind and to the right of the green and the bunkers make a low running shot a daunting possibility. If I had decided on the tee not to go for the green in two, I would want to hit a full approach shot from a distance that took the trees out of play.

Scoring
Zone
Strategy

MARK'S SCORING ZONE STRATEGY

With a five-stroke lead coming to this hole the year I won THE PLAYERS Championship (1988), my tee shot landed in the right rough. I could have heroically tried to reach the green in two, but I decided to lay up to 115 yards. This allowed me plenty of room to fly a full wedge over the trees, and I made an easy par.

In that situation, my errant tee shot dictated a change in scoring zone strategy in the midst of playing the hole. In this case, I already know before teeing off that I want to lay up 110 yards from the hole.

This is the area I want to play my approach shot from. While it is nearly 30 yards farther back from the blocked spot, I have 35 yards of fairway width to work with and plenty of room for my ball to climb over the trees.

In the distance, you can see how the fairway narrows and the trouble I avoided. This is a great example of how sometimes not hitting the ball closer to the green is better!

HITTING THE LAYUP

Learning good strategy is relative to scoring zone improvement. Knowing I want to hit wedge from 110 yards, the next step I think about on the tee is the best area to hit my layup shot from.

I decided a 150- to 160-yard shot to the layup area made the most sense. The photos below show why I made that decision.

This distance offers a wide landing area for my tee shot, and a perfect launching spot for a pressure-free layup. The next step is selecting the correct club.

A nearby sprinkler head had the yardage to the green, and I pace off the distance back to my ball. Take 2 or 3 clubs with you (inset photo) if you are sharing a cart. Don't get trapped into using the wrong club for the job because that is the only club you're carrying.

THE SCORING ZONE TEE SHOT

Playing the hole in my mind from the green back to the tee, my next decision is picking the correct club to hit the tee shot. I fade the ball, so I can relate to the 90 percent of golfers who hit the ball left to right.

- This dogleg left does not set up naturally for a fader or slicer.

- Aiming to the left side of the fairway and hoping the ball curves back brings the trees on the left into play.

- If you are not going for the green in two, why take a chance of going down the tree line to compensate for a slice or fade?

PLAY TO YOUR STRENGTHS

- You may be shorter off the tee with a 3-wood, but it brings into play the fairway where it is widest.

- Hit an easy layup from this lie to the yardage and position that provides the best shot to the green.

LEAVE YOUR DRIVER IN THE BAG!

Most players can hit a 3-wood straighter than a driver. Playing conservatively to the middle of the fairway is a higher percentage shot.

PAR 3 SCORING ZONE STRATEGY

The 17th hole at TPC Sawgrass is one of golf's most famous par 3s and a great example for scoring zone strategy. This island hole is only 135 yards from tee to the green, but I'm sure you've seen the problems it causes the world's best players during THE PLAYERS Championship. Keep these things in mind when playing a par 3:

- We don't always play at the hole on a par 3.

- Play to the safest part of the green and sneak up on the hole.

- I should be arrested if I ever play to anyplace other than the center of the green on this hole, except when the pin is cut on the left front.

MARK'S PAR 3 TIPS

I'll show you how to play this hole. While most par 3s aren't island greens, there are similarities in strategy and in picking landing areas.

1 The first thing I want to determine is the distance to the pin.

2 My next concern is the topography of the green, especially around the pin.

3 I want to know the wind direction all the way to the green.

CHECK THE WIND

Wind does not have much effect around the tee, where your ball is traveling its fastest. Instead of tossing grass into the air: check the wind on the water; look at the tops of the trees; study the trees near the hole; look at the flag.

KNOW YOUR LANDING AREA

Typically, you want to putt from below the hole, but nobody in their right mind is going to try and land the ball between the bulkhead and the flagstick. My aiming point is the slope about five yards beyond the hole. The slope acts as a backboard and feeds the ball down to the hole. Select a club that allows a full shot for that distance.

SUNDAY'S NOTORIOUS PIN PLACEMENT

As you watch THE PLAYERS Championship on Sunday, you see players land the ball in the center of the green and watch as it rolls down to the pin. This is planned, and is a good example of our scoring zone strategy.

- Firing at the pin is risky because it brings the bunker and the water on the right into play.

- Good strategy requires knowing the distance and wind conditions to aid club selection.

- Always check a yardage book for exact distances to specific landing areas on the green. Factor in tee placement yardage.

- The yardage book shows contours to help you aim at a responsive landing area.

AIM FOR THE CENTER

There is more room to land safely in the center of the green. Good scoring zone players do not challenge the odds. I guarantee you will always be ahead on the final score.

PUT THE GREEN TO WORK

To illustrate how contours on the green can help your shot, I've tossed a ball in the center of the green in the same direction it would arrive from the tee. See how the slope brings the ball down to the hole. Knowing the topography of the greens is a great scoring zone aid.

INSIDE-THE-ROPES STRATEGY TIPS

Here is a selection of strategy tips to help you in the Scoring Zone. Playing the game successfully at the professional level requires looking for anything that can give you an advantage.

Incorporate these ideas into your scoring zone strategy the next time you play. Consistently hitting good shots in the scoring zone is a result of planning, as well as awareness of the subtleties of the course you are playing.

VISUALIZE SLOPING GREENS

Skilled players look for any advantage when selecting a target for approach shots. The ability to pick up the subtleties of slopes in a green is a major advantage for scoring zone play. All greens have some slope to help water run off.

It always helps to rely on a mental image to pick out the slope of the green to determine which way the ball will roll. The late Payne Stewart once demonstrated for us a great way to pick out subtle sloping. Here's his tip:

TOSS A PAIL OF WATER

Payne Stewart suggested developing the mental image of tossing a pail of water on the green, along the path you want the ball to roll. The water accumulates on the lower end of the slope. Balls tend to roll in the same direction as water would flow.

Grass Growth Direction

Knowing the direction the grass grain is growing on the green helps determine the shot to hit. It also is a factor in club selection because it affects distance.

• Grain growing toward you stops the ball faster.

• Grain growing away from you encourages the ball to release after landing.

KNOW THE TYPE OF GRASS ON THE GREEN

• *Bermudagrass greens usually grow in the direction of the setting sun. The exception to this rule is on a slope, where Bermudagrass grows in the direction the water runs off.*

• *Bentgrass greens grow in the direction the water runs off.*

• *The smooth side of the cup is with the grain.*

• *The ragged edge of the cup is against the grain.*

FOUR WAYS TO STOP A BALL

There are four ways to stop a ball on the green. The first three ways are shown here, the fourth on page 27.

1 Trajectory: Balls with a high trajectory will drop steeply on the green and stop within a few feet of where they land.

2 Spin: All balls have spin after impact. The backspin checks the ball on the green. Applying greater backspin on a soft-covered ball will cause it to spin back.

3 Roll: A ball that is hit lower and allowed to roll onto the green will stop within a specified distance.

4 Backboard: The fourth way to stop a ball is to hit a slope that acts as a backboard. The ball hits the slope and rolls back down the hill, hopefully toward the pin. If the pin is above a slope, factor that in when deciding on the shot to hit. Sometimes it's easier to hit a shot that runs up the hill, while at other times a high trajectory shot works best.

CHECK UPCOMING PIN PLACEMENTS

- While walking between greens and tees, you usually have a chance to see a green you will be playing a few holes ahead. Remember where the pin placement is.

- The next pin placement may even be visible while you're traveling down the fairway.

- Upcoming greens may be visible from the tee box of the hole you're playing. Notice topography that can aid your approach shot on those holes.

YARDAGE BOOKS

Yardage books are sold at pro shops. TOUR players use detailed books during tournaments to help provide the exact yardage to hazards, to the green from various locations, and for other pertinent information.

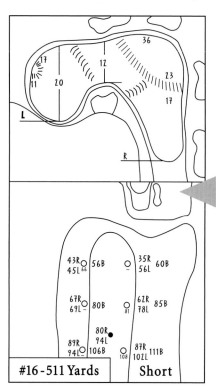

This example shows the contours of the green. Even if you play the same course all of the time, use a yardage book like a pro.

YARDAGE MARKERS

Yardage markers can vary, so acquaint yourself with them early in your round. Most courses have 150-yard markers, such as posts, trees or sprinkler heads. Double check them with your yardage book for the exact distance. Remember: You need to know the distance to the hole, and designate your targeted landing area.

ALWAYS CHECK THE WIND

Bruce Fleisher is always checking the wind. While you can't change it, you can adjust your alignment and shot selection to compensate for it. Here are some things to look for:

• Check the wind direction in the tops of trees. This is the area where the ball will be doing its flying.

• Check to see if the wind is strong enough to blow the pin in a certain direction. That's a strong wind.

• Check the flag to see the direction the wind is blowing on the green.

LEARN HOW FAR YOU HIT YOUR CLUBS

Successful people know every detail about the tools of their trade. For example, a dentist knows the correct drill burr to use when attacking a cavity, and a plumber knows the correct wrench size to tighten a pipefitting.

Professional golfers know the distances they hit each of their clubs. Experience and practice teaches us these nuances. The easiest way to find out how far you hit each club is to take 15 to 20 of the balls you play with, and find an open area (photo above). Then:

• Hit the balls into the field with a club.

• Eliminate the farthest and shortest ball.

• Pace the distance off to the middle of the shot pattern (arrow). This is your average distance for that club.

HOW TO MEASURE VARIOUS CLUBS

Hit the pitching wedge, 9-iron, 7-iron on up, skipping the club in between. You should see a pattern for each club. For instance, if you hit your pitching wedge 120 yards, figure your 9-iron will go 130. Usually there is a 10- to 12-yard difference between each club.

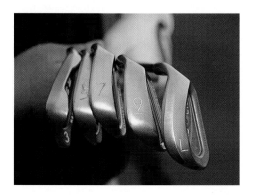

• When you're calibrating club distance, *always* use the balls you play with. Range balls are constructed for durability, and will provide a false reading.

• When you are pumped up, you have to figure additional distance for the club you've chosen.

Scoring
Zone
Strategy

3 SCORING ZONE ACCURACY: THINK GAP!

Driving off the tee presents a wide fairway to work with. But as you get closer to the hole, your target dramatically shrinks and may well be surrounded by hazards. The ball needs to track toward the target to eliminate wasted strokes. As you enter the "Scoring Zone," our professionals begin their instruction with a few basic fundamentals needed to improve accuracy.

Good fundamentals provide the keys for squaring the clubface to the ball and target line at impact, ensuring an on-line shot. These fundamentals are easy to overlook as you address the ball, so try a simple tip as a reminder. After selecting your target, remember the word **GAP** (**G**rip, **A**lignment and **P**osture).

Bruce Fleisher and Tom Lehman begin by showing you their **G**rip. Bruce then works on **A**lignment to the target and demonstrates good **P**osture for longer approach shots.

And at the end of this chapter, Martin Hall's Practice Tee features drills you can do at home to make your **GAP** strategy consistently reliable.

GRIP

Bruce Fleisher.

Grip the club correctly and you have taken the first important step toward scoring zone improvement. Some pros and low-handicap players utilize a strong grip for full shots and a weak left-hand grip for partial shots. In this book we call that partial-shot grip the "finesse grip." Martin Hall will help you master the finesse grip at the end of this chapter.

BRUCE'S LONG-APPROACH GRIP

Wearing an older glove to show where the shaft fits, I begin by laying the shaft diagonally across the fingers of my left hand. Notice that my palm is lower than the butt of the club. The glove's dark spot in the palm shows the area that will wrap around the shaft.

After I've closed my left hand, notice how my thumb extends slightly on the inside of the shaft. Tom Lehman prefers his thumb more on top of the shaft. Grip the club lightly at this point.

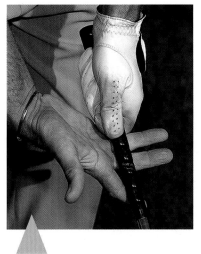

As the fingers of the right hand take their position, notice how the shaft rests on the fingers. A common mistake is to grip the club in the palms of the hands. By holding it lightly in the fingers of both hands, you are treating the club gently, like the fine instrument it is.

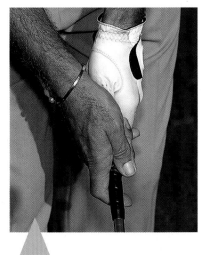

This is how the grip looks when both hands are closed on the shaft. Pay special attention to the V's formed by the thumb and forefinger of each hand. The V's of the left hand look like they're pointing toward my left shoulder, but it's the glove material that makes it look that way.

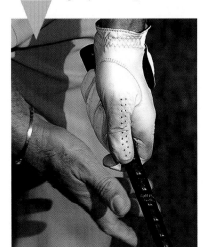

BRUCE SAYS:

Many golfers mistakenly believe the terms "strong grip" and "weak grip" refer to grip pressure. A strong or weak grip is identified by the position of the hands on the club, not by how tightly it's held.

A strong grip, used in the long game and for full shots, has the V's formed by the thumb and forefinger pointing toward the right shoulder. In a weak grip, the V's point more toward the middle of the body. The finesse grip is a weak grip and is ideal for partial shots. It promotes a high slice spin, which stops the ball quickly. This is perfect for the short game, but terrible for the long game.

By inserting tees in the V's you can see they really point toward the inside of my right shoulder. Before implementing the grip change, my left hand used to be weaker.

The tees should be pointing to the 1 o'clock position when looking down at your grip. When I changed my grip, I strengthened the left hand, moving it slightly right. The stronger left hand provides additional distance without a loss of control.

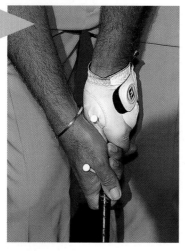

This is an overlap grip. I prefer to rest my right pinkie on top of the finger instead of in the groove. Jack Nicklaus prefers to interlock his pinkie with the second finger of the left hand. This particular grip works best for me. Experiment and refine your grip to improve your game.

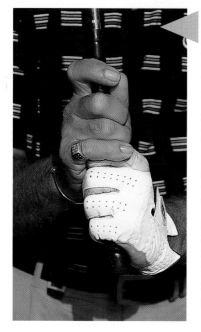

TOM'S WEAK GRIP

I always use the same grip—a strong right hand and weak left hand—for both full and partial shots. That means the V of the right hand points toward my right shoulder and the V of the left hand points more toward the center of my body (arrows above).

Try not to have a lot of tension in your grip. Instead, concentrate on developing a relaxed feel. I try to feel the tension in the third and fourth fingers of both hands. I hit a lot of balls, and when my grip pressure feels wrong I'll take my thumbs off the club and hit balls to get the pressure correct.

THUMB ON TOP: TOM LEHMAN

Notice how my left thumb is on top of the shaft when the club is held out parallel to the ground? In this view you can also see the butt of the club extending beyond my palm. Never grip the club all the way to the top of the grip.

ALIGNMENT

Alignment is the second prerequisite for scoring zone accuracy. Here on the practice range you can see the ball taking off and tracking toward the pin. The balls on the green show my consistent shot pattern, thanks to the proper **GAP** and swing plane.

Consistency is the operative word. Good scoring zone players hit shots consistently because they take the time to set up correctly. Repeating a good swing is much easier when you have solid fundamentals to rely upon. Aligning your body parallel to the target line is a must for accuracy.

CHOOSE A SPECIFIC TARGET

Always choose a target. Without one, how can you correctly align your body to a specific target line? Try these alignment tips:

- Stand behind the ball to identify your target.

- Lay a club down that runs parallel to the target line. Because your toes will be aligned with the club, be sure to point it to the left of your target. (If you point it at the target, your shot will end up to the right.)

POSTURE

Posture is the final element of the **GAP** way of thinking. As you address the ball along the parallel target line, your posture plays a pivotal role. Maintaining a good spine angle, head position and flexed knees will allow the body to rotate around a constant axis. At this point, you want to make sure the feet, knees, hips and shoulders are parallel.

My good alignment and posture promote an accurate swing plane. Bad posture requires compensations throughout the swing. Forty years of playing golf provide the answer as to which is more effective: Take the time to get your posture right for each and every shot.

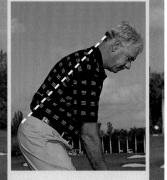

SPINE ANGLE

The spine angle I establish will be maintained throughout my swing, which allows my arms to hang down normally without making any adjustments. Notice that my chin is away from my body.

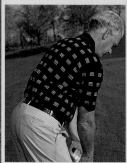

PUSH DERRIÈRE BACK

Push your derrière back to set the hips properly, which helps you make a proper on-plane hip turn.

PRACTICE TEE

Welcome to the Practice Tee. Do you know why TOUR players are so precise from 80 to 150 yards out? Simply put, they control the direction and distance of their shots extremely well.

The direction the ball goes is influenced by the plane of the swing and where the clubface is at impact. Distance is related to both impacting the ball in the center of the clubface, and club speed. This is something TOUR players do very well but TOUR Partners Club members may have trouble with.

The profile of a good scoring zone player consists of:

1 A neutral setup at address. Our starting point.

2 A good swing plane. (Covered in Chapter 4.)

3 Good timing to allow the body, arms, hands and club to be in the right place at the moment of impact; another great reason to move on to Chapter 4 after this Practice Tee lesson.

SCORING ZONE GRIPS

The best all-around players often use two grips. They may change their grips intuitively, but change they do. Try thinking of it this way:

STRONG GRIP

FINESSE GRIP

When making a full swing, use the same grip you use when driving the ball. As you look down, the V's of both your hands should be at 1 o'clock, and pointing between your right shoulder and your chin. This strong grip is good in a full-swing situation because it tends to close the face slightly, helping square the clubface at impact.

When making a partial swing, weaken your grip and turn your hands so the tees are pointed more to the top of the shaft. Take some time to experiment a bit, moving the tees between the 11 o'clock and 12:30 positions. This finesse grip is good in a partial-swing situation because it creates a desirable slice spin that stops the ball quickly.

STRAIGHT-SPINE SETUP DRILL

For a scoring zone shot, you don't want to be behind the ball hitting up. That is the short-game death move. The setup position needs to facilitate a downward impact at the bottom of the swing arc.

As you set up, your spine should be straight when viewed from the front or back, compared with the right spine tilt that promotes sweeping the ball when driving. Try this drill to help develop that feeling. You will need a stick about the length of a shaft as an aid. A yardstick will work just fine.

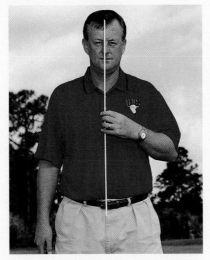

1 As you set up, imagine a line that bisects your forehead, nose and spine. Hold the stick up as I have to get that feeling.

2 Hold a club across your chest by your shoulders so that it forms the letter T with the stick. The club should be parallel to the ground.

BEND FROM THE HIPS DRILL

With the body erect, the next step is to properly set the posture. A stick inserted in the shaft-end will help position the club properly as you bend down from the hips.

This is a neutral setup, with the shaft pointed between my arms. Don't push your hands forward for this short-game shot. Usually when you do that the body counterbalances it by tilting back, causing you to incorrectly hit up on the ball.

1 In your non-tilted setup, hold the stick on the shaft, pointing the stick toward the center of your body. As you bend from the hips down to the ball, the hands will be in a neutral position.

2 The stick is pointing directly between my arms. The slight right shoulder dip is normal for a right-handed golfer. My weight is balanced evenly.

3 To help arrive at this position, think about taking a bow. After all, you have just mastered the GAP.

4 100 TO 150 YARDS

ENTERING THE SCORING ZONE

After you have advanced your ball to within 150 yards of the green, it should take only three additional strokes to get the ball into the hole. Following this math, 54 strokes from within 150 yards for an 18-hole round is a realistic goal. Once you improve in the "Scoring Zone," more accurate and properly executed approach shots can eliminate additional strokes.

Of course, this sounds great in theory, but you still must hit the ball, so we will begin our trip through the scoring zone with instruction on how to execute shots from 100 to 150 yards out. These are primarily full-swing shots.

Bruce Fleisher invites you to join him inside the ropes for a closeup look at his swing, and then he demonstrates how to escape trouble. Tom Lehman executes a shot over difficult terrain. And on the Practice Tee, Martin Hall helps you develop the swing plane of a pro.

Let's begin. Stroke elimination is underway!

BRUCE'S LONG APPROACH SWING

Bruce Fleisher.

The 150-yard marker indicates the distance to the center of the green. But is it 150 yards to the pin? The pin placement is fairly close to the front of the green, which means the pin is more like 140 yards. A 10-yard difference affects club selection and, in this case, if I didn't make adjustments, would have left me with at least a 30-foot putt coming back.

Calculate your distances carefully, adding or subtracting yardage for pin placement or your desired landing area.

Off the tee on the shot that follows, I want my ball to finish toward the left side of the fairway, which provides the best angle to fire at the pin. My ball flight pattern is mostly straight because, in my opinion, today's equipment is not conducive to working the ball in different directions. When I have to manufacture a shot to escape trouble, then I work the ball for either a draw or fade. But this shot is a straight 8-iron to the pin.

FOCUS ON A TARGET

I always focus on a specific target and then visualize the shot (as shown) that I want to hit. With the pin in the front of the green, I want to hit a shot with a high trajectory that will stop where it lands.

SET THE GAP FOR ACCURACY

Selecting the pin as the target provides the reference point for an accurate setup. After *Gripping* the club properly, I *Aligned* my body parallel to the target line I've chosen and set my *Posture*. *GAP*, that simple three-letter acronym, makes this easy to remember.

BRUCE SAYS:

The phrase "working the ball" refers to the flight pattern a ball takes after impact. A "draw" for a right-handed golfer is a controlled right-to-left path, while a fade is a controlled left-to-right path. You can work the ball in either direction by altering your setup and swing to put the desired spin on the ball. Sometimes severe ball path adjustments (hook or slice) are needed to escape trouble.

ADDRESS

Without wind to worry about I can aim straight at the pin. If you normally cut or draw the ball, factor that ball flight into your aiming point. I suggest using the Practice Tee drills at the end of this chapter to develop an accurate swing plane.

When in the fairway within reachable distance of the green, don't squander your position by doing something silly on the next shot, like setting up haphazardly. Finding a cure for an inconsistent swing may be as simple as working on fundamentals at address. Deviating from the fundamentals can require compensations to get back to the ball: compensations that will throw your swing off plane and ensure an off-line shot.

My head is behind the ball and will be the axis for my swing. My chin is away from my chest, allowing room for my left shoulder to swing under it.

This is a normal shoulder tilt for a right-handed golfer.

My long game grip is the same one used for this shot. The V's of both hands are pointed inside my right shoulder.

My stance is less than shoulder-width apart. My left foot is slightly open. After 40 years of golf, I don't think about this. If it feels right to me, I go with it.

For consistent results, the ball should be lined up with the left armpit. This is the bottom of the swing arc and the point at which the clubface squares to the target line at impact.

BACKSWING EXTENSION

The club must be on plane to impact the ball accurately. Hip high to hip high are critical positions in the swing for this to occur. The Practice Tee (starting on page 62) demonstrates drills to help get your club in these accurate positions on the backswing, downswing and follow-through.

The hands, arms and shoulders lead the turn away from the ball, and remain linked together in a triangle. The hips resist the turn, instead of leading it, and build the torsion that releases into a powerful, effortless swing.

A wide swing arc will be established in the extension. Notice that I'm not "reaching back" to the point that would shift me out of balance. The weight is being transferred to my right leg. Wherever the weight goes, power follows.

My shoulder turn is beginning to pivot around my steady head. The head will move slightly toward the back of the stance. The key is that it feels steady to me. Too much head movement is a symptom of swaying.

This clearly shows the triangle relationship between the arms and chest. Maintaining this linkage is critical to a good swing. To remain connected, you want the butt of the club in front of the chest during the swing.

My weight is transferring to my right side, and I feel it build in my right instep. If I stopped my swing in this position, I wouldn't be able to lift my right foot, but I could easily lift my left foot. Transferring weight to the left side on the backswing, a common mistake, is called a reverse pivot. Check yourself.

s I swing back through to the hip-high position, the importance of aligning myself to a target becomes obvious. Keeping the club on plane without adjusting for direction results in a shot that will be on target.

The reason TOUR players' swings look so fluid is that we keep everything simple. We don't make mid-swing compensations, and the clubhead is free to allow the power of centrifugal force to dominate.

As the club reaches this backswing position, staying on plane keeps the shaft pointed just inside the ball. Maintaining a proper swing plane during the backswing makes it easier to return to the ball on plane, producing an accurate shot.

This is a good checkpoint for the swing. As you take the club back, the butt of the club should be pointing between the parallel target and foot lines to stay on plane. A player's height will vary the swing plane, but the club's butt must still work between these lines. As you swing back, check where the butt of the club is pointing.

- If the butt points to the left of the foot line, the backswing is too steep.

- If the butt points to the right of the ball target line, the club is behind you, causing a backswing that is too flat.

When you practice, lay a club on the ground in front of the ball, pointing toward the target, and another on your parallel foot line.

TOP OF THE BACKSWING

As I reach the top of my backswing, my body is fully coiled and ready to release the club back to the ball. Even as a SENIOR TOUR player, I'm able to maintain a straight left arm. Many club members may not have my flexibility, but try to keep your arm as straight as possible to maximize the width of your swing arc.

I did not bring the club back to parallel, but it is far enough back to allow all of the timing elements to come together on the downswing. A backswing that is too short makes it difficult to coordinate the arrival of the body and the club-face to the ball at the same time.

My wrists are fully cocked. Having a relaxed, tension-free grip allows the wrists to cock naturally. Any tension inhibits the free-flowing motion a swing must have.

A big shoulder turn is important to the success of a long approach shot. The shoulder turn produces a wide swing arc to travel back, down and through the ball.

My head has maintained its centered position and I'm winding up over my right leg, feeling the weight in the right instep. Weight is energy, and I've stored it on my right side.

Notice my hip position. I began the swing with my hands, arms and shoulders in a one-piece motion. Because they are linked together, they pulled my hips into the back-swing. Some golfers incorrectly allow their hips to lead the backswing.

To develop the backswing torque needed to powerfully release the stored up energy, the hips turn only as far back as the upper body pulls them. The hips' resistance to making a full turn produces torque, which translates into power when released through the ball.

This photo makes it easy to see my swing plane back to the ball. All I had to do was set up correctly and swing back. Can you see how coiled I am?

The link between my hands, arms and chest continues to the top of my backswing. All three must stay linked together throughout the swing to create the distance and accuracy a good scoring zone player needs.

This photo clearly shows the importance of keeping your chin away from your body at address. See how my left shoulder has rotated under my chin? If my chin were too close to my chest, my left shoulder would have bumped into it, knocking the swing off plane and limiting the length of my backswing.

Notice that my hips did not over rotate on the backswing. The wrinkles in my shirt show how coiled my body is.

I still have flex in both knees, but you can see the right leg has remained slightly straighter than the left. This shows the weight has correctly shifted to the right side.

Your back should be facing the target at the top of your backswing. Notice the hip position.

DOWNSWING TRANSITION

The transition to the downswing begins with the hips taking the leadership role. They should start turning back toward the ball just as the upper body reaches the top of the backswing (see inset below).

Remember that correct weight transfer follows the hands. When my hands moved toward my right side, my body's weight followed. Now as my hands begin moving toward the ball, the weight begins transferring over to my left side.

The shoulders are drawn into the downswing by the lower body turning back toward the ball. If you start your downswing with your arms, you will come over the top, causing either a pull or a slice.

The hips lead the return to the ball. Compare this main photo to the inset photo, above, of my backswing . See how my hips have moved, and pulled my upper body into the downswing?

As the transition begins, the weight has started to shift toward the ball.

My body is powerfully uncoiling, led by my hips. As my left arm reaches a position parallel to the ground, it remains extended, keeping the swing arc wide. Amateurs are in awe at how far pros can hit certain clubs. The reason: Our wide swing arcs enable clubhead speed to develop naturally.

See how I'm maintaining the relationship between my hands, arms and chest? This linkage is vital to an accurate shot. Notice how close my right elbow is to my body. Notice that my hips lead the way (inset shot).

DOWNSWING

The club shaft is pulled down to a position parallel to the ground as the upper body continues following the hips back to the ball. Some amateurs look like they're chopping wood in this position, the result of throwing the club outside its plane.

I want the club to follow a powerful inside track, squaring at impact and then returning to the inside and continuing on to the follow-through. The time it takes for the club to go from the top of the backswing to the completion of the follow-through is a half-second. In that brief time, you can't control the positions the club goes through. All you can do is set the stage for a good swing, and trust it.

The link of the hands, arms and chest continues through the downswing. Notice that my elbows, and other body parts, are not flying away on their own. It's an economy of movement.

The hips continuing turning toward the target. A critical timing element is that the hips must turn through the impact area *before* the clubhead arrives.

My weight is still moving over to my left side. You can see the left leg is clearly reacting to the weight transfer.

The clubhead is approaching the ball from the inside and perfectly on plane. The wrists have not prematurely released. I don't make a conscious effort to release my wrists; instead, I allow centrifugal force to take care of that.

By the way, if you've noticed a pink band on my wrist, I have to admit to being a little superstitious. I wore that at a tournament I won, and hated to cut it off. Who am I to anger the gods of golf!

IMPACT

Impact is a fluid position, with the club passing through the impact zone at maximum power. Visualizing impact past the actual point the ball and clubface meet eliminates prematurely stopping your swing.

The clubface arrives square to the target line, propelling the ball directly on line. Every swing you make in the scoring zone must have accuracy as its primary outcome.

The triangle shows that the link of my hands, arms and chest has been maintained through impact. A straight line can be drawn down the right arm into the shaft. The wrists have not released.

These two views show what occurs at impact. A good ball-striker's divot occurs after impact. Notice how the ball starts up as the clubface is making a divot, proving my swing plane brought the clubhead down to the ball, rather than impacting it on the upswing.

The downward swing imparts backspin on the ball, producing the high trajectory I need to stop the ball after it lands on the green.

A ball will start out in the direction the shoulders are pointing. Because mine are parallel to the target line, the ball starts on target.

The hips have cleared, providing plenty of room for the arms to swing through. Any blockage moves the swing off plane.

The clubhead arrives at impact slightly inside and on a downward track.

100 to 150
Yards:
Entering
the
Scoring
Zone

51

FOLLOW-THROUGH

My swing's momentum carries it through to a complete follow-through. See how my right arm rotates over the left, keeping the club on plane? Shoulder rotation pulls my head up as the follow-through progresses, while the weight shifts completely over to my left side, and I finish facing my target.

These two photos represent an outstanding view of how I finish my long approach to the target. This shot requires proper distance and accuracy.

The extension of my arms maintains a wide swing arc as I follow-through to a complete finish. My swing is consistent, which is why I selected an 8-iron; I knew it was the correct club for the distance.

Accuracy is a result of the swing plane. When the clubhead follows the correct path, it arrives at impact in the correct position—square to the target line.

100 to 150
Yards:
Entering
the
Scoring
Zone

WHEN THE WIND BLOWS

Golf is seldom played under ideal conditions. On the SENIOR TOUR, playing in wind is unavoidable. Players will not force a shot when conditions or pin placements make that a risky proposition. We have an arsenal of shots to rely upon that may be more appropriate for the situation.

HOW WOULD YOU PLAY THIS SHOT?

It's a sunny day in South Florida, but the wind is blowing into me where I stand. Yet the palm trees behind the green show a strong right-to-left wind. The pin is tucked behind a large bunker, and the green drops off to water on the left. What shot would you play? Make your decision before moving on.

1 A high shot that lands softly?

2 A layup shot?

3 A low iron that runs after landing?

BRUCE'S CHOICE

The high-percentage shot in this situation would be a low iron that releases after landing. Compare the two photos below to see the difference in trajectories. With a wide landing area, plenty of room to run the ball and a backboard behind the green, I want the ball to land and release.

A high trajectory (smaller photo) subjects the ball to the swirling winds, so my key is to lower the ball's flight (larger photo at bottom). The shot should bore through the wind and release after landing.

BRUCE'S LOW-TRAJECTORY APPROACH

All scoring zone shots require the same GAP fundamentals (Grip, Alignment and Posture) with an on-plane swing. Here are tips to consider to play this low-trajectory shot correctly:

• Take an additional club. If the shot is normal 8-iron distance, choose a 7-iron instead and play the ball slightly back in your stance.

• A three-quarter swing will get the job done.

1 Wind blowing at you produces a higher trajectory if you swing too hard. Solution? A smooth, three-quarter swing. Here's how to do it. Choke slightly down on the club because you'll be playing the ball slightly back in your stance. Adjust your alignment for the wind (compensating either slightly right or left). And at address, have 60 percent of your weight on the side closest to the target; this means a right-handed player will have more weight on his or her left side.

2 The overall swing should be a mirror image. Here is the proper three-quarter backswing you should be making. Remember: this isn't a full-swing situation!

3 Swing through and make sure your follow-through is a mirror image of your backswing; this three-quarter follow-through will maintain the rhythm and timing of your shot. Hold your club a little firmer with your left hand through impact.

PUNCH SHOT

When you're between 100 and 150 yards from the pin, you may encounter a situation where a tree ahead blocks a lofted approach shot to the green. This is when you want to hit a shot you are comfortable with, rather than relying on luck. My suggestion: Practice the punch or knockdown shot.

- From 145 yards, I choose a 5-iron (inset).

- Less loft is important because I will not be making a full swing.

- I want the ball to stay under the branches, land about 25 yards short of the green, and roll toward the pin.

BRUCE'S PUNCH SHOT

Slightly choke down on the club. I play the ball opposite my left armpit, but you may want to position the ball slightly back in your stance, depending on the trajectory you want. To help with distance, visualize the ball going under the branches and rolling to the green after landing. Hit to the landing point.

Your hands and clubhead do all the work, so remain steady as you take a half normal backswing. This is one case where a tighter grip helps—by restricting the wrists. A common mistake is to sway forward as you begin the downswing.

All golf swings require rhythm and timing. A rushed shot would lead to sculling this shot, instead of allowing the 5-iron loft to work for you. At impact, the clubhead arrives at the same time as my hands, arms and shoulders. The ball will start on a lower trajectory than my 8-iron did from 150 yards.

This finish position is the mirror image of my backswing. Note that the hands should be opposite the face, and the blade of the club should point toward the target.

Fairway Bunkers

In the scoring zone, fairway bunkers are found between 100 and 150 yards from the hole. This is one of the toughest shots to get close. Hitting the ball fat and leaving it in the bunker is a typical result for many amateurs.

The key is not to try to explode the ball out of the bunker. Pick it out. From 100 yards and out and with a trailing wind, I'm using my 53-degree Callaway A-wedge.

BRUCE'S FAIRWAY BUNKER TIPS

Setup

Choke down on the club slightly to compensate for your feet being lower than the ball in the sand. Remember to play the ball back in your stance; this encourages impact with the ball before the sand. Notice that my weight is on my left side.

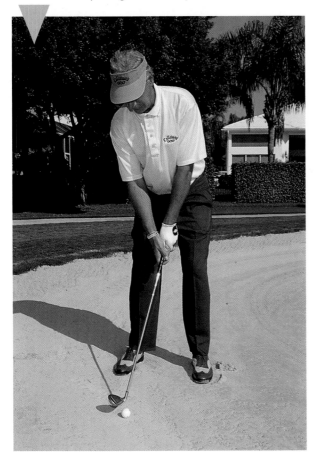

Pinch the Ball

The clubhead pinches the ball and picks it off the sand. At this moment of impact, you can see that the clubhead has only slightly entered the sand after impact. Don't explode the ball out as you would in a greenside bunker.

The Swing

This is a cautious and calculated swing. Be sure to stay centered throughout the swing. Also, keep your head still and rotate around it as you swing. Through it all, swing with tempo and rhythm; you are picking the ball off the sand, not exploding it.

BRUCE'S PRACTICE SWING TIP

Before stepping into a fairway bunker, try this 3-step tip to develop the feel of picking the ball off the sand:

1 Look for a small leaf outside the bunker.

2 Practice picking the leaf off the grass with your swing.

3 Step into the bunker and repeat the same swing.

100 to 150 Yards: Entering the Scoring Zone

APPROACH OVER DIFFICULT TERRAIN

This scoring zone shot is on a 145-yard par 3 hole. It requires flying the ball to the green. When facing shots like this, put the terrain out of your mind and concentrate on reaching the green. If it helps, visualize grass all the way to the hole. Concentrate on the green to improve your chances of reaching it. If you think about the rocks or water, sure enough that's where you'll end up.

STAY ON PLANE

These photos show the importance of a good swing plane to ensure an accurate shot. Accuracy, and choosing the correct club for the distance, are paramount in landing on this green. The Practice Tee (page 62) comes up next with some drills to groove your swing.

These tips should help you with shots that require higher lofts:

• Think about finishing high with your follow-through.

• Always finish facing your target to make sure you completed your follow-through.

PRACTICE TEE

SWING PLANE

Both Bruce and Tom emphasized that scoring zone accuracy is derived by developing the correct swing plane and then repeating it every swing. You don't need a perfect swing, but the ball can only go to the target if you meet the following requirements:

1 You must hit the ball in the middle of the clubface.

2 As the ball leaves toward the target, the clubface must be square to the target line.

3 The club must be swinging in the correct direction from hip high to hip high to send the ball on line to the target.

Are you a member who has never understood this or given it much thought? You are not alone, since most amateurs don't have a clear picture in their mind of how all this comes together. But you will after reading this chapter's Practice Tee.

ARE YOU A CENTER HITTER?

Begin by checking where you hit the ball on the clubface. This can be done on the practice range.

I'm spraying my clubface with "On The Mark," a powder available at golf specialty stores. You also can use pressure strips that fit on the clubface. Talcum powder also works.

IN THE CENTER

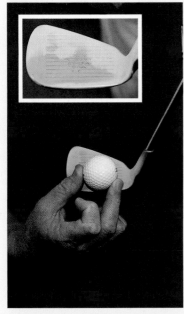

You want to impact the ball in the center of the clubface. If you are a center hitter, the powder will reveal a ball mark in the center of the clubface.

TOE HITTER

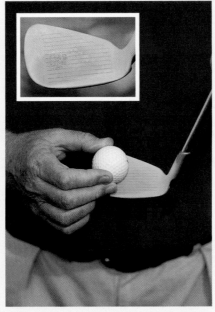

This is the mark of a toe hitter. If your normal shot pattern is short and right, this is where you are incorrectly hitting the ball. If you feel the club is turning in your hands at impact, the reason is that it was knocked out of your hands because you hit the ball on the toe.

HEEL HITTER

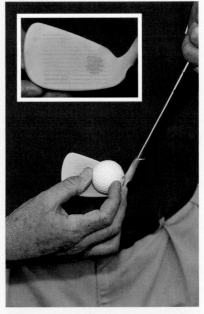

If you hit the ball off the heel of the clubface, this is the mark you will see. When you hit a short iron off the heel, it will usually go to the left because the club turns around the ball. Hitting the ball with the shaft causes a shank to the right.

THE GATEWAY DRILL

This backyard drill (below) will help train you to become a center hitter. Buy some large colored tees from a golf specialty store or paint some Popsicle sticks. Greg Norman used this drill as a junior golfer.

1 Stick a tee in the ground where the middle of your clubface will be. Place a second tee in the ground just off the toe and a third at an angle off the shaft. You have just built a gateway!

2 Address the center tee and swing. A correct swing will hit only the tee in the center.

3 Hitting the farther tee is equivalent to hitting the ball on the heel.

4 Hitting the inside slanted tee is the equivalent to hitting the ball on the toe.

IMPROVING YOUR SWING PLANE

Accuracy comes from where your swing plane is on the downswing from hip high to hip high. If you can form a mental image of this, you will become a better scoring zone player.

Here I'm using a teaching aid to illustrate proper positioning. A number of swing training devices are available to develop this feeling. Perhaps your practice range has an aid you can use.

Look at the photos below to develop the swing plane concept in your mind, then refer to Bruce Fleisher's long approach swing to see how they apply.

100 to 150 Yards: Entering the Scoring Zone

SPINE ANGLE DRILL

Keeping your head on a pillow is Ken Venturi's wonderful swing thought that will help any golfer. This pillow drill will help develop that feeling as you maintain your spine angle throughout your golf swing.

I built a practice station out of PVC pipe. It has a padded board on one end of a horizontal pole. The pole connects to a vertical pole that I anchor to the ground. You also can put a padded board on the end of a pole and have a friend hold it while you practice.

1 To set the correct spine angle, I address the ball and then tilt from the hips forward until I lightly touch the padded board above my forehead. My head is the center of the swing circle. Practicing this drill will make you more consistent.

2 While keeping my head on the board, I make a swing where my hands go from shoulder height to shoulder height. I want my head to remain in touch with the board to maintain the correct spine angle.

3 It's okay for the head to turn on my follow-through. Use this drill and the Gateway Drill at the same time, to improve your spine angle and center hits with one swing.

SQUARE THE CLUBFACE DRILL

Swinging a weed cutter not only helps produce a weed-free lawn, but it can help develop the feel of a square clubface at impact. The large, thin cutting section allows you to concentrate on squaring the blade at impact.

You can readily see if the blade is square, or the toe or heel is arriving first. If you don't have this tool, a broom works just as well.

1 Begin by addressing a weed using the fundamentals you have learned so far. For those lucky individuals without weeds, plain grass is fine. Try to clip the grass at the same point every time. This is the bottom of your swing arc.

2 Take the weed cutter back to the hip high position on your backswing.

3 As you swing down, the cutter should return to a square position at impact. You should see it arrive slightly open, square at impact, and close after impact.

4 Swing through to a hip-high position on your follow-through.

5

50 TO 100 YARDS
MID-RANGE

This chapter could have been titled "The Wedge Symphony," because within the 50- to 100-yard area of the "Scoring Zone," wedges are the primary instrument played. Amateurs have a love/hate relationship with wedges, but professionals play them as sweetly as a Stradivarius. Bruce Fleisher and Tom Lehman are our wedge virtuosos in this chapter. Bruce opens with insight on distance control, and then Tom takes over and demonstrates how to hit wedges from various lies. On the Practice Tee, Martin Hall presents some drills to keep you linked during your swing.

LET THE CLUB DO THE WORK

When a professional makes three or four birdies in a round, at least two are set up by wedges. Yet, for most amateurs, wedges may be the least appreciated, understood and practiced clubs in their bags.

Perhaps TV adds to the confusion. Viewers see us pros play wedge shots and don't know what to think. Sometimes we finish high on our follow-through and sometimes we don't. Sometimes we have a short backswing and sometimes it's longer. But every wedge shot has one constant—it must be struck solidly.

KEY: PARALLEL ALIGNMENT

My feet are parallel to the target line in my 9 o'clock backswing. Even though distance is the topic of the moment, accuracy also should be uppermost in your mind for scoring zone shots. Some players prefer to open their stance and adjust their setup accordingly.

BRUCE'S 9 O'CLOCK BACKSWING

How important are wedges to my game? My practice time is devoted almost entirely to them, because improved wedge play is an important reason for my success on the SENIOR TOUR.

I normally use the same swing for my three wedges. I control the distance with club selection.

The key to achieving consistent distances with my wedges is the backswing. Nine o'clock is the magic number I want my arms pointing at on this arm-dominated backswing. I make a normal follow-through and finish facing the target.

50 to 100 Yards: Mid-Range

Tom's Three Wedges

Here are the distances I can count on for my wedges:

- Pitching wedge = 125 yards (full swing)

- Sand wedge = 105 yards (full swing); 85 yards (three-quarter swing)

- Lob wedge = 67-70 yards

Lob Wedge　　　Sand Wedge　　　Pitching Wedge

Tom's Wedge Philosophy

Developing correct distance control is vital for wedge shots from 100 yards and in to the pin. Billy Mayfair explained how to determine your club distances in Chapter 2. I would add that you should also measure your scoring zone clubs for three-quarter swings.

I'm comfortable hitting three-quarter shots with my 7-iron through my wedges. With a three-quarter sand wedge, I can swing smoothly and hit it 85 yards with outstanding control. However, between 55 to 70 yards, it's difficult to control distance with a sand wedge because shortening the swing can negatively affect rhythm and, in turn, the consistency of your shots.

As a result, many players carry a third wedge—the lob or "L" wedge. This 60-degree club allows more of a full swing. Accurate distance control is the result.

WORKING THE BALL

Drawing the ball from right to left works great for most of my shots. But once I have a scoring club in my hand, my thoughts turn to hitting a fade. I feel distance control is more consistent with this left-to-right shot.

SETUP FOR A FADE

The keys for hitting a three-quarter fade:

- Aim left of the pin and play the ball forward in the stance.

- Set up far enough left so you can turn through the ball and hang on with your hands.

SETUP FOR A DRAW

The keys for hitting a three-quarter draw:

- The ball should be farther back in your stance and you should choke down slightly to compensate.

- Aim more to the right.

50 to 100
Yards:
Mid-Range

95-YARD SAND WEDGE

How would you play this 95-yard shot to a double-tiered green with the pin located on the upper level? A backstop on the green's back edge completes the contouring.

TOM'S CHOICE

This is a good example of why it's important to know the firmness of a green. Just hitting any shot is not the way to become a good scoring zone player. Green firmness determines the shot selection. Forcing a shot to a green that won't accept it is a tactical error.

This green is soft, so my plan is to hit a sand wedge to the backstop, allowing the ball to feed back toward the pin. Since the pin is just over the ridge, it would be a low-percentage shot to fly it on the ridge and stop it short of the hole.

I'm setting up to hit a fade. My feet are open to the target line and the clubface is aimed slightly left of the pin. For a fade, I position the ball slightly forward in my stance.

The three-quarter backswing helps control distance. I want mostly arm movement in the swing, and only limited lower body movement.

DOWNSWING

Downswing begins the crucial hip-high to hip-high positions Martin Hall demonstrated earlier in the book. To hit a fade, I try to match this position past impact.

PAST IMPACT

This is almost a mirror image of my downswing hip-high position. Notice how my right arm has not rotated over my left, as it would to hit a draw. This is "hanging on to the club with your hands" I referred to on page 71.

FIRM GREEN SHOT

The green here is soft. But this is how I would have hit the shot if I knew the green was firm:

• Slightly close the face of the sand wedge.

• Hit a low draw that lands on the front edge of the green.

• Play a low trajectory shot that allows the ball to release and run up the hill.

—Tom Lehman

95 YARDS: FROM THE ROUGH

The ball is 95 yards from the same double-tiered green, but it's in the rough. How would you play this shot?

TOM'S CHOICE

The key to this shot is knowing how to read the rough. You have to decide if the ball is going to come out hot, or muffled and soft. You learn this from experience.

READ THE ROUGH

When there is grass between the clubface and ball, the shot will not have a lot of backspin. This means it will be "hotter" coming out of the rough and will release a greater distance after landing.

My shot selection has to be a three-quarter punch shot to the front of the green, letting the ball release to the hole.

To start a three-quarter punch shot properly, keep your setup slightly open, with the ball back in your stance. Put slightly more weight on your left side. Also, be sure to choke down on the club.

IMPACT

Your left-hand grip pressure needs to be slightly firmer to keep the clubhead from turning as it powers through the grass. The loft of the sand wedge will propel the ball into the air, if you continue accelerating through the shot.

TOM'S ROUGH TIPS

- Grass between the ball and clubface brings the ball out hot, so plan on letting it roll.

- A clean lie allows you to put backspin on the ball, which stops quicker.

- The condition of the rough can change. In wet grass, the ball comes out softly, but when the rough dries and gets crispy, the ball will come out hot.

PUNCH FOLLOW-THROUGH

Keep your hands opposite your face in the finish position. With punch shots, the clubface should finish pointing at the target. You can see the lower, hotter trajectory.

50 to 100
Yards:
Mid-Range

90 YARDS: UPHILL LIE

The fairways are beautifully contoured here at the DC Ranch outside of Phoenix, and provide a perfect site for this uphill, 95-yard shot. How would you play it?

TOM'S CHOICE

This uphill lie encourages a lofty shot, but my personal preference is not to allow the ball to get too high. When that happens, I feel like I've lost control to the elements. Instead, I'll play another adaptation of the punch shot, taking a less lofted club and making an easier swing .

Hitting a sand wedge from this uphill lie would propel the ball too high, so I selected a pitching wedge with less loft. Notice that the ball position is back in my stance, and my shoulders and waist are parallel to the hill's slope.

I tend to hook the ball from an uphill lie, if I swing too hard. To eliminate this high and left tendency, I make an abbreviated backswing and try to be smooth while staying in balance.

This lie offers plenty of elevation, and my downswing brings the club into the ball along the ground line. The less lofted pitching wedge compensates and will launch the ball on a lower trajectory. Notice how my shoulder and hip lines match the slope.

IMPACT   **FOLLOW-THROUGH**

Following the fairway contour eliminates digging the club into the hill. I still take a divot after impact. Keeping my swing smooth is the key to remaining in balance.

After impact, my hip line still matches the slope (left photo). And after the ball has left the clubface, you must achieve follow-through in a fraction of a second to achieve the lower trajectory you want. My hands are opposite my face and the clubface is pointing at the target (right photo): the ideal finish for this punch shot.

50 to 100
Yards:
Mid-Range

60 YARDS: DOWNHILL LIE

You already know that a downhill lie makes it difficult to get the ball airborne. How would you play this downhill, 60-yard shot?

SHOT DETAILS

- Select a 60-degree lob wedge.

- Play the ball back in your slightly open stance.

- Aim left of the target and open the blade. Whenever the ball is played back in the stance, you take loft away. Opening the blade adds loft back.

- My weight is on the left foot. This takes the legs out of play. The more lower body movement you have, the greater your chance of skulling the shot or hitting it fat.

TOM'S CHOICE

Getting the ball into the air is the prime consideration from this downhill lie. You can do several things to encourage a higher ball flight. One is to set your shoulder line to match the slope.

BACKSWING	DOWNSWING	PAST IMPACT

My backswing illustrates that this is less than a full shot. Notice how my blade is pointing to the target. Smoothness eliminates excessive body movement that will destroy the chance of sliding the club under the ball. This partial backswing helps keep my legs out of the shot.

My body remains quiet as I swing the club down to this hip-high position. I remain in balance and, as the swing continues, the clubhead will follow the slope and slide under the ball.

Compare this photo with the downswing photo at left. Can you see how I've matched the two positions? I slid the clubhead under the ball and then extended down the slope. The weighting on my left side kept me in balance.

FOLLOW-THROUGH

My follow-through finishes high as I face the target. A high follow-through encourages a high trajectory. The ball is gaining altitude and will land softly on the green. Remember that trajectory is one way to stop the ball.

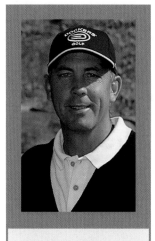

TOM SAYS:
A WORD OF CAUTION

With a 60-degree wedge, opening the blade adds bounce to a club that already has quite a bit. This can cause the club to skid off the ground, skulling the shot. It's important to know how much bounce your clubs have and to choose the type of equipment that can help your game on the courses you play.

50 to 100 Yards: Mid-Range

60 YARDS: LIE BELOW YOUR FEET

How would you play this 60-yard shot when the ball is below your feet? Good scoring zone players can readily adapt to any lie, but you have to practice to become proficient.

TOM'S CHOICE

When the ball is below your feet, it wants to drift to the right. I have a solution for that problem. I play the ball back in my stance, choke down, aim 10 feet to the left and let it drift.

This becomes an easier shot because by turning I'm actually hitting more into the hill. Another slight change: I don't want to bend at the knees at address. Bending from the waist helps maintain the correct amount of knee flex and keeps my weight more on my heels.

Maintaining my balance is vital to hitting this shot properly. The three-quarter swing allows me to swing the lob wedge smoothly and stay on plane.

The lob wedge approaches the ball and prepares to slip under it. Allow the natural loft of the club to do the work for you, instead of helping the ball into the air.

IMPACT

FOLLOW-THROUGH

If you follow the clubhead's path, you can see by turning left at address how the path is slightly more into the hill. This is a fairly easy shot to hit, and I allowed for the ball to drift back toward the right.

I maintained my balance through the swing and finished high to encourage a higher ball trajectory. My right foot usually pivots and points toward the target in my follow-through, but as a result of additional weighting toward the heel, it slightly rises to indicate weight transfer.

50 to 100
Yards:
Mid-Range

50 YARDS: LIE ABOVE YOUR FEET

With the ball above your feet, the tendency is for the shot to go from right to left. My most common mistake is trying to compensate by combating the lie with a left to right fade. Wrong! How would you play the shot?

TOM'S CHOICE

I've learned from my mistakes to let curvature work for me on this shot. Try anything else and the hill gets in the way. On a fade, the hill is higher than the ball, so when the club comes from the outside in to put spin on the ball, it runs into the hill. A fat shot is the result.

PLAY THE CURVATURE

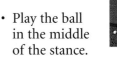

- Choke down on the club to compensate for the ball being above your feet.

- Play the ball in the middle of the stance.

- Rock back and forth until feeling a balance you can maintain.

- Make a partial swing and slide the club under the ball following the contour.

- Finish with your hands opposite your face; this movement will help you remain in balance throughout the swing.

PRACTICE TEE

After viewing some outstanding swing tips by Tom Lehman in a variety of situations, can you determine the one common characteristic for each shot he hit? Bruce Fleisher mentioned it in the beginning of the chapter. The answer:

You have to hit every wedge shot solidly. This requires timing the body parts to arrive at the ball together. Timing is keeping the hands, arms and body in sync. You have *improper* timing if:

1 Your body is too fast for your arms. The club lags too far behind and you tend to push the ball or hit it thin.

2 The club is too fast for the body. The result is bladed and hooked shots.

TOWEL DRILL

The towel drill helps you link your arms with your body by developing the triangle Bruce Fleisher maintained throughout his swing. If you pick the club up, this drill will stop the arms from running away from the body on the backswing.

This drill is not for a full swing but is ideal for the 9 o'clock and three-quarter swings discussed.

Fold a towel so that it fits between both arms and your chest. Address the ball and make 9 o'clock and three-quarter swings. The ideal finish position for this drill is with your hands opposite your face: the same follow-through Tom demonstrated for punch shots.

Notice I transfer my weight and pivot my feet as I normally would do. This also is a good warmup drill to instill that linked-up feeling before you head out on the course.

6

10 TO 50 YARDS
PITCH FOR SUCCESS

"**C**oach" Billy Mayfair is your guide in this chapter. He will demonstrate the ins and outs of hitting pitch shots to the green from 10 to 50 yards. On the Practice Tee, Martin Hall offers drills to transform you into a "major league" scoring zone player.

Ten to 50 yards is an important range to master. As Billy points out, this is the "must" area of the scoring zone. Once you're within 50 yards, you must get as close to the hole as you can or even make the shot. A positive shot-making attitude is important to the outcome. Visualize your shots going into the hole instead of just getting close.

Between 10 and 50 yards your margin of error dramatically shrinks. Proficient scoring zone players select the correct club and execute the proper shot from this position. All too often a less-skilled player chooses the wrong club and hits a high shot when a low one would

have been better, and vice versa. We'll start by looking at three pin placements from 20 yards off the green.

PLAY IT LIKE A PRO

When you're 10 to 50 yards from the pin, planning out and trying to visualize your shot becomes paramount. Three factors will determine the success of your shot—the club you choose, the trajectory you give the ball, and where the ball lands. These three factors are listed on the chart at right.

In the picture below, Billy Mayfair has three different pins in front of him. How would you play each shot—club choice, ball trajectory and landing area? Copy the "How Would You Play It" chart at right, to organize and write down your decisions. After you decide how you would play the shot for each pin, turn to pages 87-89 to see how our coach would do it.

HOW WOULD YOU PLAY IT?

Close Pin:

CLUB	TRAJECTORY	LANDING AREA

Middle Pin:

CLUB	TRAJECTORY	LANDING AREA

Far Pin:

CLUB	TRAJECTORY	LANDING AREA

PICK CLUBS YOU TRUST

Getting the ball close to the pin from this distance is imperative. I would choose among three wedges from 20 yards, but my selection would change from 10 yards off the green (Chapter 7).

For executing pitch shots, limit your club selection to a few clubs that you trust, depending on the shot. Maintaining a positive attitude is important. Knowing these are your "go to" clubs from this area bolsters confidence. You don't want to be indecisive in the Scoring Zone.

BILLY'S CLUB CHOICES FOR PITCHING

(Left to right) 61-degree lob wedge for close pin; 56-degree sand wedge for middle pin; 48-degree pitching wedge for far pin.

LOB WEDGE TO THE CLOSE PIN

A high trajectory with a soft landing is the solution to stopping the ball near the close pin. From 20 yards there is enough distance for the ball to go high and land softly, so I selected a lob wedge. Choosing to run the ball in this situation would be unpredictable.

• A lob wedge propels the ball higher the longer your swing.

• My backswing will be the longest for this close shot, versus what it would be for the sand and pitching wedge shots on pages 88 and 89.

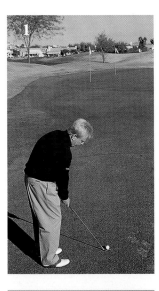

SAND WEDGE TO THE MIDDLE PIN

With more room to land the ball between the fringe and the middle pin, I'll select my sand wedge.

• I can fly the ball longer and land it on a larger area.

• The lower trajectory allows the ball to release and run the short distance to the pin.

PITCHING WEDGE TO THE FAR PIN

With a lot of green to work with I selected my pitching wedge because it has less loft and provides more carry.

• Pick a landing area midway on the green and on the path to the hole.

• The ball will release after landing and run to the pin.

MASTERING THE LOB WEDGE

The lob wedge is a difficult club to hit well consistently ... for both amateurs and professionals. It requires a big swing, and how the ball comes off the clubface out of the grass is always questionable.

But the results are rewarding, if you hit the shot precisely. I'll demonstrate how to effectively hit the lob wedge for shorter and longer pitches, but the only way to build confidence is through practice. When the pressure is on and this potent scoring zone club is in your hands, you want plenty of "hands-on" experience behind you.

THE SHORT PITCH

When pitching with a lob wedge, improper hand positions can cause problems. Typically the hands are either too far forward or too far back.

I've seen less-skilled players hitting 50-yard pitch shots with a lob wedge with their hands behind the ball. The result is a short, high shot that goes right. For this shot, the hands need to be a little forward.

SETUP

Use the finesse grip (page 36) and a slightly forward shaft angle, with a narrow but slightly opened stance and a forward ball position. The club should be aimed at the target. Keep your weight slightly to the front, because partial swings like this allow only limited time to transfer weight back and through.

BACKSWING

Employ a longer backswing. This is necessary when you're using the 60-degree loft club, to create enough clubhead speed to use the lob wedge properly. Try different backswings as you practice; this will help you develop a feeling for both the height and distance you can produce, depending on your backswing.

CLUBHEAD PASSES BALL

After impact, the ball will run up the face of the open-faced lob wedge. This will cause trajectory to go up as well as forward—a good combination for this shot. Stay connected through the shot, almost as if you're carrying that ball right to the hole. See the Practice Tee's "Beach Ball Drill" to help develop this feeling.

FOLLOW-THROUGH

Your follow-through length depends on the distance of the shot you're taking. The longer the shot, the more you need to follow through (to get more distance and height). Of course, don't over-compensate and follow through too much, or you'll over-shoot your target and have to go lob-in from the other side of the green.

10 to 50
Yards:
Pitch for
Success

91

LONGER LOB WEDGE

I can hit my lob wedge from up to 70 yards, so this 60-yard pitch is well within range. The high trajectory will stop the ball quickly after landing. Increasing my swing length regulates the additional distance needed to reach 70 yards.

Remember: Greater backswing length equals increased clubhead speed, which equals increased distance.

SETUP

Set up with a shoulder-width stance. The ball should be opposite your left armpit, to encourage a high trajectory. Align yourself parallel to the target line. Finally, be sure the club's shaft angle is neutral.

BACKSWING

The length of your backswing depends on the distance you need, with a longer backswing producing a longer shot. At the top of your backswing, your back should be to the target and your clubhead pointing toward the target.

IMPACT

At impact, your clubhead should be accelerating under the ball. Notice the loft of the clubhead as it points toward the target at impact.

FOLLOW-THROUGH

Complete your follow-through to assure maximum clubhead velocity at impact. Use normal weight transfer through the swing, and finish facing the target.

LOB OVER TROUBLE

You may be tempted to hit a running pitch shot over this bunker and let the ball roll to the pin. But if you look at the contour of the green you'll see that it slopes away past the hole, so your running shot will keep on running.

Good scoring zone players want to lob the ball over the bunker and have it stop close to the pin. My good friend Phil Mickelson wrote the book on shots like these. Have you watched him and wondered why he takes a full swing to go such a short distance? I'll show you.

SETUP

The key to a good lob: how you open the clubface. The more you open it, the higher the ball will go and the less distance it will travel.

At setup, open the clubface so it's almost flat. Choke down on your grip. Open your stance but aim the club at the target. Position the ball far forward (which encourages higher trajectory). Swing along your foot line.

BACKSWING

IMPACT

Don't do a full backswing. But do transfer your weight properly, and stay connected to the ball.

The ball is lagging behind the clubhead because it's gaining height with a minimum of forward motion. The open clubface, created at setup, was maintained by swinging along my foot line. The photo on the right was shot at a slower camera speed to show the clubhead in motion as it follows that path.

10 to 50 Yards: Pitch for Success

PITCH AND RUN SHOTS WITH TOM

Billy has demonstrated the versatility of the lob wedge in pitching. Clubhead loft and a forward ball position, both of which allow the club to slip under the ball at impact, produce a high trajectory that helps stop the ball.

For middle- and far-pin placements, he mentioned using sand and pitching wedges to carry the ball to the green on a lower trajectory and let the ball release and run after landing. We'll show how to do just that.

You may prefer hitting an 8- or 9-iron for the same pin placements. The principles are the same, but be sure the ball does not come in too low and hot or it will run through the green. Choose a landing area in front of the green as long as the terrain won't kick your ball off the target line.

TOM SAYS:

To keep your trajectory lower, select a sand wedge, pitching wedge or another short iron. Your distance off the green and pin placement dictate club selection.

- More loft equals higher trajectory equals less release.

- Less loft equals lower trajectory equals more release.

SETUP

BACKSWING

Encouraging lower trajectory starts at your setup. Billy recommends selecting a sand wedge, and then using a finesse grip that is choked down slightly (because the ball is farther back in your stance). Feet should be close together. The club shaft is angled forward.

Billy's left arm and wrist are more vertical with this shot than with the lob wedge. This less-lofted clubhead ensures a lower-trajectory shot. On the lob wedge shot (page 91), the ball lagged behind at this point; here, it's ahead and lower.

TOM'S BALL RELEASE SWING KEY

IMPACT IS THE KEY POSITION

- Notice how my hands are ahead of the ball at impact, de-lofting the club.

- The ball will fly to the green but on a lower trajectory.

- Landing less steeply allows the ball to run after landing.

- Pick your landing spot and determine the amount of run you want before selecting your club for the shot.

FOLLOW-THROUGH

FINISH

Billy's left arm and wrist are more vertical with this shot than with the lob wedge. This less-lofted clubhead ensures a lower-trajectory shot. On the lob wedge shot (inset, from page 91), the ball lagged behind at this point; here, it's ahead and lower.

Billy finishes this lower trajectory shot about waist high. His feet do not pivot toward the target as they would on full-swing shots.

10 to 50
Yards:
Pitch for
Success

CHANGE YOUR TRAJECTORY

Want to lower your trajectory to allow the ball to run even longer after landing? Try this:

CHANGE BALL POSITION AND YOUR CLUB

- Select a pitching wedge.

- Play the ball farther back in your stance.

- Choke down because a ball farther back is not the lowest point in your swing arc, and the ground comes up sooner.

PRACTICE TEE

CREATING SPIN

The scoring zone shots in this chapter must create ball spin to be successful. Good scoring zone players have the feeling of cutting across and underneath the ball. That's wonderful for the scoring zone game, but very bad for long shots.

- If you've played racquet sports, you'll recognize the same feeling

when hitting a slice spin shot.

- Your racquet cuts across and under the ball, sending it high. Whether it goes short or longer depends on the racquet angle at impact. In golf, the impact angle is set by the club loft you select.

- In golf, if the ball had legs you would want to cut them off!

PADDLE CUT DRILL

This is a drill to help you understand the feeling of cutting across the ball, helping you re-create the feeling you want to achieve when

hitting these scoring zone shots. Other drills here will develop the actual feeling even further.

Mount a tennis ball on a pole about waist-high (1). Using a ping-pong paddle, take swings at the ball (2). Cut across and under the ball (3), sending it high. This is the feeling you want to generate when creating spin on your scoring zone golf shots.

DEVELOPING SPIN

If you want to execute your longer pitch shots with Billy Mayfair's consistency and accuracy, we need to remove an incorrect moving part from your swing—the wrists.

Too much wrist action hurts your swing, unless you need to create a lot of spin on the ball for very special shots, which we'll discuss in Chapter 8. But for now let's quiet those wrists down.

BEACH BALL WRIST DRILL

For a 50-yard wedge shot, too much wrist movement will take the club too far to the inside and around the body on the backswing. Thinking that you want to swing straight to the target incorrectly causes this inside action. The only thing you want going to the target is the ball.

This beach ball drill will help correct the inside problem. Unlike the towel drill that helped you stay connected, the beach ball makes sure that you do not swing your arms too much around your body on the backswing.

INCORRECT WRIST MOVEMENT

CORRECT WRIST MOVEMENT

DOING THE DRILL

Place a large, partially inflated beach ball between your upper arms. Grip the club with the finesse grip demonstrated in Chapter 3. Use a wedge and play the ball in the middle of your stance, making a three-quarter swing. Keep the beach ball in place between your upper arms.

LEFT HAND OVERLAP DRILL

Scooping or trying to lift the ball into the air is a problem common among less-skilled scoring zone players. You don't need to help the ball into the air. That's what the high-price technology does.

This drill helps eliminate the "scoops." Do this drill periodically as a form of maintenance to prevent bad habits from creeping in. Finding this drill difficult to do is an indication you probably need to do it more often to correct the problem.

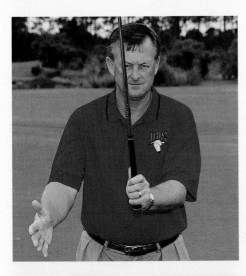

1 Grip your club in front of you with your left hand.

2 Wrap your right hand over the left.

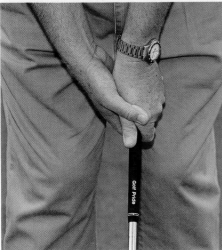

3 Take your normal stance with the feet slightly apart.

4 Simulate hitting a 50-yard pitch shot, and then hit some real balls to eliminate helping the ball get airborne.

10 to 50
Yards:
Pitch for
Success

AVOID THIN SHOTS DRILL

INCORRECT SHOULDER IN THE AIR

As you are swinging through the ball, you want your left shoulder going around to the left and not just going up in the air. If you hit thin shots or hit them to the right, this drill will quickly turn you around.

1
2
3
4

Holding your left shoulder with your right hand prevents the shoulder from going up in the air after impact. The pressure on the left shoulder keeps it going around to the left: The perfect finish position for slicing across these scoring zone shots!

DRAW YOUR PITCH

This is an advanced player's shot but a good one for everyone to practice. When you have a back left pin with a lot of green to work with, and a hazard slightly encroaching on your line, a draw shot will get you close.

This right-to-left shot starts the ball lower and, as the ball lands, it will kick to the left and run toward the pin.

For the ball to draw, make the clubface close to the target line when impacting the ball. The way to play this shot is to train yourself to make a forearm rotation.

WATER BUCKET ROTATION DRILL

Everyone has this teaching aid. All you need is a partially filled bucket of water. Do not make the bucket too heavy. Concentrate on emptying it behind your left shoulder.

1 Partially fill a bucket of water (far left photo).

2 Stay connected through the impact area as you begin to throw out the contents (middle left photo).

3 Rotate your right arm over your left to follow-through, tossing the water behind your left shoulder. This is the same rotation feeling you need to develop a draw pitch (near left photo).

SMILE AT THE BALL DRILL

Some members are too tense when they play these delicate scoring zone shots. I have the perfect cure: smile at the ball, like I am doing in the photo at right.

You have to relax your muscles to smile, which in turn relaxes the muscles in your neck, which stops you from tensing up.

Here are a few ideas to keep in mind, to keep you relaxed throughout your shot. Just smile all the way through your shot (top photo). Or hum in a single note all the way through your shot. But my favorite technique is from a Scottish pro. Say "Alexander Cuddogan," Alexander on the backswing and Cuddogan all the way to the finish (photos above). Say it properly and it will pace your swing while relieving your tension.

10 to 50 Yards: Pitch for Success

103

HITTING LOB SHOTS: CLUBFACE POSITION, ALIGNMENT, SWING

When you hit a lob shot you want to hit it high and you want the ball to stop quickly. You need two ingredients, if you want to hit this shot consistently.

• You need to open the clubface.

• You need to lay the club back.

This demonstration will help your understanding of how this shot needs to be played.

SQUARE CLUBFACE

When the clubface is square, it points to your target.

OPEN CLUBFACE

When you open the clubface, it points to the right of the target.

LAID BACK CLUBFACE

Laying the clubface back flat points it less to the right but still requires a body alignment adjustment to square the face back to the target line.

ALIGN YOUR BODY LEFT

While maintaining your grip on the club, align your body to the left to get the club back on line and pointed at your target.

SWING ALONG YOUR FOOT LINE

Swing along your foot line to maintain the open clubface through impact.

HIGH SHOTS REQUIRE BIG SWINGS

A big swing will make your flop shot soar high. Clubhead speed needs to be generated because you are only propelling the ball high in the air but not very far.

Think in terms of hitting only a thin bottom piece of the ball as the club slides under it. A good tip is to concentrate on hitting just the bottom dimple (photo below). And—swing slowly but completely.

A big, full swing is important for getting height on the ball. Swing slowly but completely.

LOB BALL TOSS DRILL

This drill develops the feeling of creating a high lob shot.

1 *Hold the top of the grip with the palm of your left hand, pressing the club against the ground. Place a golf ball in the fingers of your right hand.*

2 *See how high you can throw the ball into the air without allowing your left hand to come off the club. Pretend there is a 10-foot wall in front of you and you have to throw the ball over it.*

3 *You will notice it takes good footwork to throw the ball. Likewise, it takes good footwork to hit a high lob.*

CHOP THE LEGS OFF DRILL

I've saved the most graphic drill for last. Earlier I mentioned wanting to chop the legs off from under the golf ball for the higher lofted shots. This is the perfect drill to help you visualize sliding the clubface under the ball.

Tee a ball high enough so a club can pass under it. Open the clubface, adjust your alignment, and make a full swing. As you swing, slide the clubface under the ball and hit only the tee: If the ball had legs, you just chopped them off. That's the key—hitting the tee from under the ball.

10 to 50 Yards: Pitch for Success

7 FIXING YOUR MISSES
CHIPPING AND SHORT PITCHES

I f you have missed the green either short, wide or long, don't panic. On average, PGA TOUR players hit the green in regulation only 64 percent of the time. So you are still in the hunt for a good score.

But with the chips on the table, professionals know how to convert misses into birdies or pars. Adopt their scoring mentality even if you are a high-handicapper: Develop a positive attitude.

A par for you is like a birdie for them, so approach these shots with a business-like attitude. Analyze the situation, decide on the strategy, select the proper club and get the job done. The great shots pulled off around the green will stick in your memory, instilling the confidence you need in the "Scoring Zone."

Billy Mayfair begins by demonstrating short pitches from 10 yards off the green, using the same three pins from Chapter 6. He shows chipping basics before launching into the actual shots and strategies.

Bruce Fleisher has a chipping formula to share, and then demonstrates a delicate touch for a fast,

downhill chip. On the Practice Tee, Martin Hall's outstanding drills help you develop the feeling you need for these close-in shots.

10 Yards Off the Green

If a wayward approach has missed the green by more than a few feet, your ability to get up and down in two strokes is put to the test. From this distance it's usually better to fly the ball over the grass than run it through, so a shorter pitch shot should be your choice.

Along with club selection, the amount of green you have to work with always plays a role in determining the shot. Using the same three pins from Chapter 6, let's once again compare our choices.

PLAY YOUR SHOT

Which club would you use, and how would you play each shot from 10 yards off the green? (See photo at left).

WHAT WOULD YOU PLAY?		
Close Pin:		
CLUB	TRAJECTORY	LANDING AREA
Middle Pin:		
CLUB	TRAJECTORY	LANDING AREA
Far Pin:		
CLUB	TRAJECTORY	LANDING AREA

BILLY'S CHOICES

To play these shots my club selections are:

• Lob wedge for the close pin.

• Pitching wedge for the middle pin, although I could use a 9-iron.

• 9-iron for the far pin, although I also could use an 8-iron.

LOB WEDGE TO CLOSER PIN

The ball is 10 yards off the green and another five yards to the hole. Here's how I would play it:

• Hit the ball a little higher so it can land softly and stop near the pin.

• Play the ball in the front of your stance to encourage loft.

• Use the biggest swing of the three shots, because the ball will go up more than forward.

• When the ball lands short of the pin it will release toward the hole.

Fixing
Your
Misses:
Chipping
and Short
Pitches

109

PITCHING WEDGE TO MIDDLE PIN

The middle pin is set 10 yards onto the green, so my shot has to go 20 yards. The keys here are to:

- Fly over the unpredictable apron grass and land the ball on the green, allowing it to run to the hole.

- Position the ball toward the back of your stance to encourage a running shot after landing.

- Practice often, to teach yourself the correct backswing length to land the ball several paces on the green.

9-Iron to Farthest Pin

With 30 yards to the hole, I need to play for more run after landing the ball on the green. My 9-iron will provide more run than my pitching wedge.

- Position the ball off your back toe to encourage release after landing.

- Choke down slightly to shorten the club; this will accommodate the back ball position.

- The shortest backswing of all three shots is the perfect length.

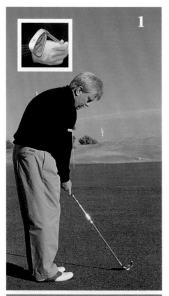

BALL POSITIONS

Correct ball position for the three pins dictates the ball's trajectory for properly executing the shots. This knowledge makes the same clubs more versatile by varying the ball position according to the shot that you need to play.

- Ball forward in the stance equals more height equals less run after landing.

- Ball back in the stance equals less height equals more run after landing.

- Always remember to choke down when you position the ball farther back in your stance.

LOB WEDGE

PITCHING WEDGE

9-IRON

A forward ball position encourages more height and a quick stop.

This ball is slightly back in the stance to encourage a slightly lower trajectory and release after landing.

This ball is positioned opposite the back toe to encourage the ball to take a lower trajectory and release even a longer distance after landing.

CHIPPING

Chipping is like putting except the ball stays in the air just long enough to go over the fringe before landing on the green. Upon landing, it runs along the same putting line to the hole.

When setting up for a chip, do you only think about getting it close? Develop a pro's birdie mentality and visualize holing it! Be aggressive and never leave a chip short. It is better to miss five feet long than five feet short; at least you had a chance at the hole.

CLUB SELECTION

My three "go-to" clubs are the 7-iron, pitching wedge and sand wedge. You should choose a combination that works best for you. Experiment with a 7-iron, 8-iron, 9-iron and the wedges, then limit your selection to three.

Practicing with a few clubs instills confidence and provides feedback to make situational adjustments and make those three clubs perform like many more clubs.

Seven- and 9-irons are prime chipping tools.

Fixing Your Misses: Chipping and Short Pitches

Billy's Guide to Improved Chipping

Good chipping starts with a good setup. Keep your feet close together but use a slightly open stance. The ball should be positioned opposite your right toe. Choke down on the club, and keep the shaft angled forward. And for a right-handed golfer: Keep 70 percent of your weight on your left side.

Backswing

Impact

The backswing is important to a good chip. Let your hands, and hands alone, take the club back; your lower body remains quiet. It will take some work to learn the proper backswing length, which will have to vary to match the shot distance.

Make sure your left wrist stays flat through impact, without releasing. Also, your hands should be ahead of the ball. And, once again, your lower body should remain quiet.

FOLLOW-THROUGH

SUCCESS

To follow-through, keep your wrists flat without releasing. Stop your swing with the club close to the ground. Once again, your lower body stays quiet.

The ball should fly over the fringe and land on the green. You have kept the swing flat so, once it lands, the ball can roll along the putting line toward the hole.

Fixing
Your
Misses:
Chipping
and Short
Pitches

115

THE LONG CHIP

With a long chip like the one pictured at right, I want the ball to land on the ground where my club is placed as soon as possible. But before selecting the club, I need to find the putting line to the hole.

FIND THE LINE, SELECT A CLUB

This shot breaks hard to the left. My first step would be to walk on the green and get a feel for the distance, before selecting a club. And then I'd bring several clubs. Don't be forced to hit the wrong club because the correct one is still in your bag. For this particular shot, I selected a 7-iron.

Set up correctly. Position the ball past your right toe, and choke down on the grip to compensate. Angle the shaft slightly forward.

On a good backswing for a long chip shot, your lower body should remain quiet. As usual, only practice can help you determine the correct backswing length you'll need to use for various shots.

To get proper impact, chip down on the ball. Keep your wrist flat through impact. The ball will quickly pop into the air along the line to the hole.

FINISH   POSITIVE RESULTS

To finish, maintain that quiet lower body past impact. Keep in mind that the chip needs to be firm and crisp to make sure the ball rolls once it lands.

The ball landed on my target spot, then rolled along the putting line to the top of the hill. At that point, I wanted the ball to start breaking left down to the hole ... and it did!

Fixing
Your
Misses:
Chipping
and Short
Pitches

BRUCE'S CHIPPING FORMULA

Bruce Fleisher.

Some of the guys on TOUR feel that the sooner they get the ball rolling on the ground the better off they will be. Sometimes I agree and sometimes I don't. It really depends on the situation. Personally, I go by feel.

Sometimes I want the ball landing quickly, while a longer carry works better for other shots. The "distance selection formula" on page 119 helps my game greatly.

For this shot, Bruce lands the ball one-third of the way to the hole.

Using the long, flat green pictured as an example, I'll explain how in this case my "one-third rule" works for this shot.

- Pace off the distance from the hole to the ball (photo at left).

- Break the distance between the ball and the pin into thirds.

- I selected a 7-iron in this case.

- For this long, flat chip I land the ball *one-third* of the way to the hole (photo below), and let it roll the remaining *two-thirds* (bottom photo) along the putting line.

- The more loft the club has, the closer to the pin you want to land the ball. I prefer landing my wedges about halfway. Practice not only helps your technique; it also builds your information base.

The ball rolls the remaining two-thirds of the distance along the putting line.

Fixing
Your
Misses:
Chipping
and Short
Pitches

119

BRUCE'S DOWNHILL CHIP FORMULA

Golf is a game of variables. Having just told you that for a more lofted club I would land it closer to the hole, this downhill run to the pin changes that. See why I said feel plays such an important role for me?

STRATEGY

With a downhill chip, I know the ball is going to release and roll.

- I decide to land the ball one-third of the way to the hole.

- Here, I select a wedge because this shot will be speedy. Plus, the higher loft acts as a momentum brake before the roll to the target begins.

- A less lofted club would create a lower, hotter trajectory and the ball would roll too far after landing.

For a good setup, play the ball off your back toe to encourage a crisp hit that imparts backspin. Choke down on the grip to adjust for ball position. Don't open the blade, because the ball is not being played forward for loft. Keep your hands forward.

To make impact, hit down and through the ball. Your stroke should resemble a putting stroke, using arms and shoulders, and very little wrist if any. Remember—don't scoop the ball! That's why clubs are built with loft. Rather, the clubface should point toward the sky, a good indication the clubface loft was positioned properly at impact. The loft will brake the momentum before the roll to the hole begins.

LANDING   **RESULTS**

This landing is right on target and the brakes are on.

I actually holed this chip on the first take. Practice using the distance formula. It does work!

Fixing
Your
Misses:
Chipping
and Short
Pitches

CHIPPING FROM THE ROUGH

This is a tough shot because the Bermudagrass found in the South is very inconsistent. When chipping from the rough, the same basic principle applies: Continue to accelerate the club after impact.

The ball is not buried (photo at right), but I'm facing the same downhill shot as in the prior example. A lob wedge is my club of choice to get the ball up and over this wiry grass.

SETUP

BACKSWING

DOWNSWING

To set up, keep your stance slightly open and choke down on your grip. Position the ball back, because the club's built-in loft is adequate to pop the ball over the grass. (This is what Billy meant when he discussed ball position and club versatility.)

Keep your backswing short, with a completely still lower body. Practice determines proper backswing length.

Smoothly accelerate the clubhead as it approaches the ball. Continue this acceleration through impact to allow the clubhead loft to launch the ball out of the rough.

Stay committed to the shot by continuing acceleration. If you flinch, the ball could be bladed or sent off-line.

Keep your wrists firm through impact to finish the shot properly. The clubface should point to the sky. See how the loft sent the ball up and over the rough.

Fixing
Your
Misses:
Chipping
and Short
Pitches

You can read about technique and strategy, but until you actually feel what Billy and Bruce are referring to, the experience will be purely academic.

I have drills to help you develop the same feelings that years of practice have instilled in the pros. But before we begin, I have one additional chip to demonstrate.

THE PUTTING CHIP

The putting chip is a very soft way to hit the ball, and is perfect for flags that are within 15 feet on fast, downhill greens. Impact is on the club's toe, softening the blow. A putting stroke is used with a wedge or 9-iron.

1 Eyes over the ball.

2 Keep your shaft vertical, like when you putt. The toe should be the only part of the clubhead touching the ground.

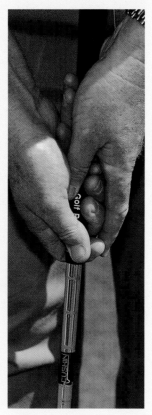

3 Use your putting grip and choke down on the club.

4 Use your putting stroke to keep impact slight and on the soft toe of your clubhead.

HANGMAN'S NOOSE DRILL

Making solid contact is your first priority in chipping. Think about contact as you read the statement below, then find a piece of rope.

Whenever you set up to the ball, there is a measurement. The measurement is from the back of your neck to the bottom of the ball. If that measurement is exactly the same at impact as it was at address, solid contact will be the result. The rope will help maintain that measurement when practicing.

1-MAKE A HANGMAN'S NOOSE

Find a piece of rope that is long enough for you to wear around your neck and hold against the shaft.

2-SET THE MEASUREMENT

Set up in the chipping address positions Billy and Bruce showed you earlier, or copy my setup if you prefer. Make sure the rope is held taut to set the measurement between the back of your neck and the bottom of the ball. Since the club will not grow or shrink as you swing, the rope measurement will stay the same, if you maintain this length.

3-MAKE THE SWING, ROPE TAUT

As you chip, keep the rope taut throughout your swing, from backswing to finish. Maintaining this taut position through impact ensures you have made a solid chip.

4-INCORRECT STROKE

If the rope becomes loose, you have shortened the measurement by raising your hands and trying to scoop the ball up as you went through impact. This is not solid contact. Keep that rope taut!

Fixing
Your
Misses:
Chipping
and Short
Pitches

ONLY THE BALL DRILL

A common mistake in chipping is thinking that if you want to chip the ball straight you have to follow-through straight. That is incorrect.

You stand to the side of the ball when chipping, so the only thing that should go straight to the target is the ball. The club should be moving to the inside after impact.

When you chip you pivot, so trying to keep the clubface pointed straight at the target through follow-through will shovel the ball off line toward the right or impact the ground behind the ball.

Place a club on the ground to indicate the target line, and two tees inside of the ball to illustrate the correct clubhead path after impact.

IMPACT

The clubhead is square to the target line at impact, and the ball begins on a path straight to the target.

IMPACT PLUS 1

The ball is still on track to the target, while the clubface is following the inside path over the first tee.

IMPACT PLUS 2

The ball stays on track toward the target, with the clubface following the inside track, and now over the second tee. Try to develop the feeling that the club is on a swing arc and comes slightly around after impact.

CLUB DESCENT DRILL

Another misconception is that you hit down on the ball for a chip shot. That's not exactly correct, as our hangman's drill proved.

- If you hit down on the ball, the rope's tightening would have provided immediate feedback with a sharp tug at the back of your neck.

- You swing down along the swing arc. This maintains the measurement demonstrated earlier.

- Try this club descent drill as a "governor" for your downward motion.

To build a practice station for club descent, place a club down so that it lines up with the outside of your right foot. Place the ball off your right toe. Set up as you learned earlier.

2-DOWNSWING

After making a short backstroke, swing down to the ball. Your clubhead should skim over the grounded club's shaft.

1-PRACTICE STATION

3-IMPACT

At impact, the clubhead swings down to the impact position at the correct angle. You can combine the hangman's noose drill with this drill to develop two important chipping components: solid contact and correct downward swing path.

EYES PARALLEL DRILL

When you set up to chip, your eyes have to be parallel to the target line. For example, think of an imaginary line drawn through your eyes and point it parallel to the target line.

If your head is tilted and your eyes are off line, you can't chip accurately. Maintain a level, parallel look at the ball.

GOOD

As seen from the ball's viewpoint, the eyes are parallel to the target line.

INCORRECT

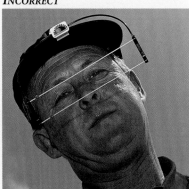

This eye line is not parallel to the target line, and an off-line scoop with additional strokes is the likely result.

Fixing Your Misses: Chipping and Short Pitches

8 CREATIVITY

"These guys are good" is more than just a passing comment to describe the players on the PGA TOUR: It's the truth, as this chapter proves. While some fans marvel at the pros' long drives and prefer watching from the tees, other fans stake out locations near the greens and usually are rewarded with exhibitions of creative genius.

This chapter will show you incredible shots from extremely difficult "Scoring Zone" lies that all golfers find themselves facing at times.

Bruce Fleisher produces two masterpieces from hardpan and pine needles. Mark McCumber demonstrates two shots from a steep downhill lie that slopes away to a lake.

Mark takes a "breather" as he demonstrates some basic sand play, and Tom Lehman hits a sharply angled uphill shot from the grass above a bunker. Billy Mayfair joins Mark to explain how the pros hit the spin shot that takes one bounce and jumps back.

This is creativity at its best. These guys are good! Here are some of their secrets.

HARDPAN

Says Bruce Fleisher: "The picture below shows a pretty good result from my lie on hardpan. The ball is taking its second bounce and actually rolled, hit the pin and went in. We don't have the picture to prove it, but trust me it did." (Author's note: "Even I am awed by the shot and watched it go in instead of shooting it." —*Steve Hosid*)

This close-up inset photo shows the Florida version of hardpan. If you have a dirt and clay base on your course, instead of sand, the ground will be hard where it's bare. The creativity begins by selecting the landing point.

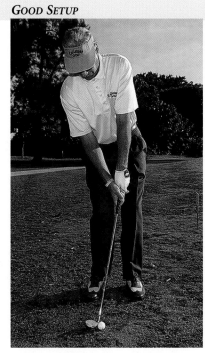

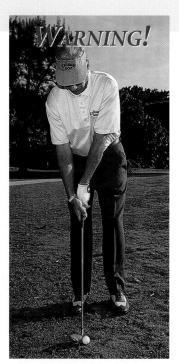

This ball is 22 yards from the pin. I select a landing site that feeds into the putting path to the hole. My landing site is on the fringe, because that fringe will scrub off some of the ball's speed before it rolls onto the green. Club? I'll use a lob wedge and aim a yard left of the hole to allow for some kick after landing.

A good setup here starts with hands ahead of the ball, with the ball positioned in the middle of your stance. I like this position because I have to get the ball up and over this terrain before it arrives at the fringe. I'm playing for some loft here … not a low punch shot.

Be careful! The shaft position in this shot is angled incorrectly back in an attempt to "help" the ball into the air. Instead, move your hands forward so that the descending blow will launch the ball for you.

THE SWING

This sequence of four shots shows the proper swing. Remember to keep your head still throughout the entire shot, which is mostly an arm swing with very little body movement. The clubface should impact the ball with a descending blow. Commit to the shot and don't hesitate or flinch: Maintain club acceleration.

Creativity

PINE STRAW

You see this shot a lot at Augusta National during the Masters and at other well-manicured courses where trees and paths near the green have pine straw mulch or pine needles around them. Assuming there is no tall grass between the ball and the green, a pitch and run is the shot you need to play.

Once you make your decision, commit to the shot. If you question yourself in golf at any time, you're in trouble.

To set up properly for this shot, keep your weight more on your left side (top photo). I can stand on one leg (bottom photo) to prove it! Ball position should be back in your stance. For this shot, I've selected my 49-degree wedge.

A proper punch swing employs a rhythmic and slow back-swing. How far should you go on the backswing? Once again, that's a part of the equation that only personal practice can determine. Swing through should be rhythmic and slow as well. The idea is to hit down and through, trying to nip the ball. Do not release your wrists as you finish this shot.

Creativity

SEVERE DOWNHILL GREENSIDE LIE

Says Mark McCumber: "Don't cringe when you see me taking this length of backswing with water just on the other side of the green. I committed to hitting this flop shot, and if you remember Billy Mayfair's lob wedge demonstration, the ball will go up higher the bigger I swing."

There are two ways I can play this shot. I'll begin by demonstrating the lob first. Here's the situation:

• Nine yards to the edge of the green.

• The actual distance to the hole is not as important as the distance to where you want the ball to land when pitching around greens.

• I have a clean lie and will be able to get the clubhead on the ball.

• I want the ball to go high with backspin that will act as a brake when it lands softly before rolling.

• It will roll past the hole, but I'll be safely on and close enough to convert the putt.

Aligning your shoulders to the slope of the hill (top photo) is the key to correctly playing this scoring zone shot. Don't make the mistake of aligning them toward the ground (bottom two photos).

For success on this shot, I opened the lob wedge clubface and my stance at address. As the clubface moves through impact (above left), it points toward the sky. I extend down the slope line, maintain the open clubface (top photo), and finish by bringing my arms around my body and up so the back of the clubface correctly finishes facing the target (above right). A clubhead that finishes pointing lengthwise to the target indicates the clubhead incorrectly rotated closed through impact—and you better get your ball retriever out.

Creativity

OPTION: SEVERE DOWNHILL GREENSIDE LIE

We are on the 18th hole at the Tournament Players Club at Sawgrass, and by now I know if I'm playing well enough to attempt the lob shot. You have to factor in all aspects before creating a shot.

Depending on the circumstances, it might be better to carry the ball over the rough, land it on the fringe and let it run toward the hole. The grass is thick, so I have to guard against the club getting stuck.

To set up for this shot, I position the ball past my right foot (photo at left); this closes the clubface to the correct loft degree (top photo). Choke down on the club (photo above) to compensate for this ball position. For this particular shot, I have selected a sand wedge. If I used a 7-iron, it would close to a 4-iron loft and I would lose the outcome I want.

THE SWING

The swing is important here. Keep your lower body very quiet, and maintain firm wrists through impact. You need to get solid impact to execute this shot properly. This advice gets you partway there. Like all the other shots in this book, practice is the only way to determine the proper backswing and overall feel you need to play each shot.

Creativity

BASIC BUNKER SHOT

A book can be written on all the aspects of successfully playing bunker shots. However, you find bunkers in the scoring zone, and good scores require an understanding of how to get out of them. The following tips will help.

A huge mistake that less-skilled players often make is gripping their club before opening it. Instead, hold the club in your fingers and open the blade, then close your grip.

INCORRECTLY CLOSED BEFORE OPENING

If you open the club incorrectly after gripping it, this is what you see: With the hands under the grip it's impossible to recreate this open position at impact.

Line A is your target line. Line B is your alignment line. Line C is your swing line. Know which is which before you let your shot go.

Creativity

139

THE BUNKER SWING

- **1** - Set up with your hands forward and your weight on your left side. Choke down to match the spot where the club enters the sand. If you stand farther away from the ball, it goes higher and softer.

- **2 and 3** - Match your backswing to the length of your shot.

- **4 and 5** - The club slides under the sand and ball. Notice how the sand is just starting to lift under the ball to propel it out of the bunker.

- **6, 7 and 8** - Accelerate smoothly through the shot to finish.

SEVERE UPHILL LIE

If your ball skips through the bunker or rolls down from the green, you can end up with this lie. Here's how I play the shot after selecting the specific lofted wedge for the incline of the hill and the distance to the hole.

SETUP

To set up properly, take a wide stance. This will keep you balanced, even if you have to stand in the bunker. Choke down to the shaft to shorten the club, and play the ball back in your stance. Preset the impact position, aligning your shoulders and hips parallel to the slope.

THE SWING

Remember—the farther down the shaft you grip, the longer your swing will need to be. Swing smoothly but make good contact and maintain a firm left side. Notice that the shoulders are parallel to the slope at the finish of the swing. Push your weight up the hill, so you finish with the weight on your left knee; this will maintain the clubface angle of attack.

Creativity

SPIN SHOT

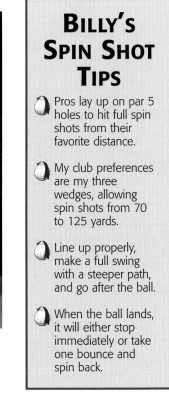

All struck balls have spin, but the shot that amazes amateurs is when the ball lands and jumps back. Here are the seven prerequisites for playing that shot.

1 A clean, tight lie.

2 A soft-covered, high-spin ball.

3 A receptive green.

4 Clean grooves on your club.

5 A big swing.

6 Impact from the clubhead that pinches the back of the ball against the ground.

7 Exceptional hand\eye coordination.

Billy Mayfair.

It takes skill to hit this shot. If you can stop the ball on the green quickly as a result of trying to master this shot, pat yourself on the back.

I'll begin by demonstrating the ball/clubhead impact relationship, and then Mark will hit the spin shot.

IMPACT

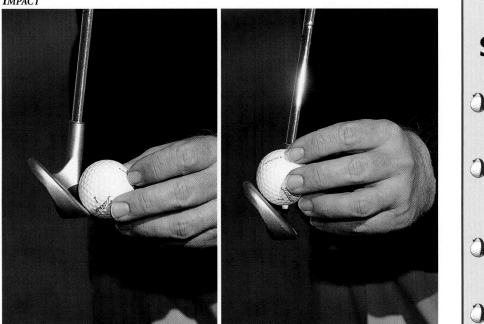

The clubhead impacts the back of the ball (left photo), pinching it against the ground. Clean grooves on the club grab the soft-covered ball, rolling it backward up the clubface (right photo) before launching into the air. This increases the amount of backspin on the ball.

BILLY'S SPIN SHOT TIPS

- Pros lay up on par 5 holes to hit full spin shots from their favorite distance.

- My club preferences are my three wedges, allowing spin shots from 70 to 125 yards.

- Line up properly, make a full swing with a steeper path, and go after the ball.

- When the ball lands, it will either stop immediately or take one bounce and spin back.

READY-SET-SPIN!

Want a tip for improving your hand\eye coordination? Try bouncing a ball on the clubface of a wedge. It's just one of the things pros do to work on hand\eye coordination, and it can help you too.

First, set up right. Notice that my ball position is slightly back from the middle (1), to facilitate the descending swing path. I take a full swing, and impact occurs after a steep descending path (2). Yes, the club takes a divot after impact (3). Good rotation during follow-through helps this shot work, as does to finish facing the target (4).

Creativity

143

9 MAKE PRACTICE FUN

This book will make you a better "Scoring Zone" player only if you practice. Golf is a full-time occupation for our four professionals. Over the years they have devoted many hours of practice time perfecting their games, and they continue practicing to maintain their competitive edge. Scoring zone shots require both finesse and feel, and practice instills the confidence needed for success. The key is to make your practice sessions fun!

Martin Hall's Practice Tee drills, featured earlier in the book, are a great guide to learn the fundamentals needed to produce good shotmaking. They teach the techniques and feelings necessary for mastering the shots.

This chapter deals with practicing hitting to targets. We selected PGA TOUR Partners Club member Andy Warden to demonstrate some target-oriented drills to make your practice fun. Plus, Billy and Bruce have a few other practice tips to pass on before you head out to the range.

ANDY WARDEN: PARTNERS CLUB MEMBER

Profile

- Owner of The Warden Company, a promotional marketing firm.

- Board member of the Arnold Palmer Hospital "Champions for Children" Committee.

- Executive director of the Golden South Classic, an elite high school postseason track meet.

- Vice president of the Bert Martin Foundation.

Business and community responsibilities limit Andy's practice time. A member of Arnold Palmer's Bay Hill Club in Orlando, Florida, he looks forward to his weekly game, and practices when possible.

We asked him to demonstrate some target-oriented practice drills that could fit easily into his schedule. But first, we corrected one serious scoring zone problem.

FIRM THE WRISTS

Andy was having chipping problems because he flipped his wrists, trying to help the ball into the air. We suggested placing a solid object, in this case a wooden spoon, into the watchband on his left wrist. A ruler also works.

As a result, he found his wrists were forced to stay firm through impact and the ball was hit crisply and stayed low. Next, it was time to move on to a target.

TOWEL CHIPPING DRILL

Chipping the ball accurately requires landing on a specified target before the ball releases along the putting path. Placing a towel a few paces on the green provides a strong visual image for aiming.

- Andy's first few balls ended short as he tried to help the ball into the air.

- We had him stand behind the ball, visualize the target area and then execute the shot.

- Using visualization, he immediately improved and landed his second attempt on the towel.

- This drill helps you develop a feel for distance.

TOWEL PITCHING DRILL

Billy Mayfair stressed ball position and club versatility. Placing towels on the ground several yards apart provides the perfect pitching practice station.

Andy is hitting balls and experimenting with different trajectories. He uses the towels as distance aids, landing the balls between them, on them or running a ball to a specific distance. Try working on these pitching basics:

• Develop a feel for distance.

• Vary the ball position.

• Vary swing length.

TOM LEHMAN DRILL

Earlier in the book, Tom told of how he practiced lobbing balls over a sign when he was a kid. Every time he succeeded, he moved closer. It's a great drill to practice while having some fun.

Andy began working his way closer to the five-foot-high fence. He cleared this close-in shot easily. You can do this in your backyard.

PRACTICE NEW SHOTS

Andy followed our four professionals' advice and began working on a *new* shot during practice, not just doing the shots he was already good at. He's seen here having pretty good success chipping a ball out of the greenside rough with his 3-wood.

Make practice sessions fun by trying to hit shots you see during PGA TOUR tournaments. Try to emulate the technique you saw and make necessary adjustments based on information you read in this book. Imagine the fun you'll have on the golf course, creating a shot in front of your friends. Little will they know that you really mastered it during a practice session.

PRACTICE EASIER AND TOUGHER SHOTS

A trap some PGA PARTNERS Club members may fall into is practicing only the shots you know you can make. The key to a good practice session is to also practice *difficult* shots.

START OUT WITH EASIER SHOTS

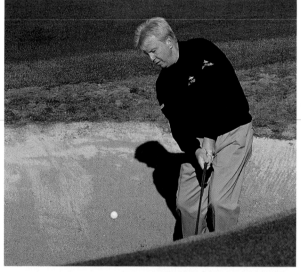 

It's okay to begin bunker practice hitting shots from good lies.

Hitting familiar shots you can handle allows you to practice technique and fundamentals.

INCREASE THE DEGREE OF DIFFICULTY

In the end though, you need to practice the not-so-pretty shots too. Here, I'm practicing a tough lie from a bunker: The ball rested in the uphill facing of the bunker.

Solution? I adapted myself to the situation and exploded it out. You need to practice the tough shots, to eliminate wasted strokes during your round.

USE YOUR CLUBS AS PRACTICE AIDS

The pros always lay their clubs on the ground for practice sessions. This is the time for even good players to reinforce the feelings that will be called on during a crucial shot in the round.

Try laying a club down as a distance aid for finding landing zones for chip shots. Move the club closer or farther as you adjust your shot and club selection.

Practice by laying clubs on the ground to reinforce alignment. Even a professional's game suffers from alignment problems, which every pro constantly works on. Use one club for the target line and the other for your foot alignment line.

10

SCORING ZONE EQUIPMENT

New materials, technology and feedback from professionals are all contributing to sophisticated equipment that is becoming readily available to golfers everywhere.

"With the equipment they have now it's like learning a whole new game," Bruce Fleisher said during a *Scoring Zone* photo shoot. Without getting carried away with the superfluous rhetoric of an infomercial, he's right!

You still have to hit the shot, but after learning and practicing the proper techniques, this new equipment can help your game take a quantum leap forward. In this chapter we show you some of the new wedge technology. But even more importantly— you'll learn how to get the most from your own equipment.

KEEP YOUR SCORING ZONE EQUIPMENT READY

Our four professionals have caddies to keep their equipment clean. Clean equipment is more than just shiny clubs; it's clean where it counts—deep in the grooves. Simply wiping your clubs with a towel will not clean the grooves that grip your ball at impact. Dirty grooves equal less spin which creates inaccurate shots.

USE AN OLD TOOTHBRUSH

This clubface looked clean, but after dipping it in water and using an old toothbrush, look what came out. The club's performance level just increased with the use of a recycled toothbrush.

Take a moment and clean your grooves after your round or at home before heading to the course. This book suggests looking for every advantage you can to become a better scoring zone player. Clean grooves are an easy advantage.

NEW TECHNOLOGY AND WHAT YOU CAN LEARN FROM IT

Visit a PGA TOUR or SENIOR TOUR tournament on practice days and head straight to the putting green. Surrounding the green are club manufacturers' reps with their bags full of wedges and putters.

Each rep must have a PGA TOUR-issued manufacturer credential before he or she is allowed to set up their display of high-tech equipment. Some reps are from major companies like Taylor Made, Callaway, Ping and Titleist, while others represent smaller, specialty companies. The reps work with the pros to help them fine-tune their equipment to their games.

5 CT. DIAMOND

Pros usually are willing to try something new during practice to evaluate its effect on their shots. They can immediately detect differences, because of their swing consistency.

Many of the golf companies take the player's feedback to their development departments and the product continues to improve. Your golf specialty store or pro shop may have some of this equipment available, but on TOUR the technology is cutting-edge and new developments are already in the works or are being refined.

DIAMOND IN THE ROUGH

PureSpin wedges feature heads that combine stainless steel and an "indestructible diamond-crystal coating" on the clubface to grip the ball. As you can see, this wedge even sparkles in the sun.

CUTTING-EDGE WEDGE DESIGN

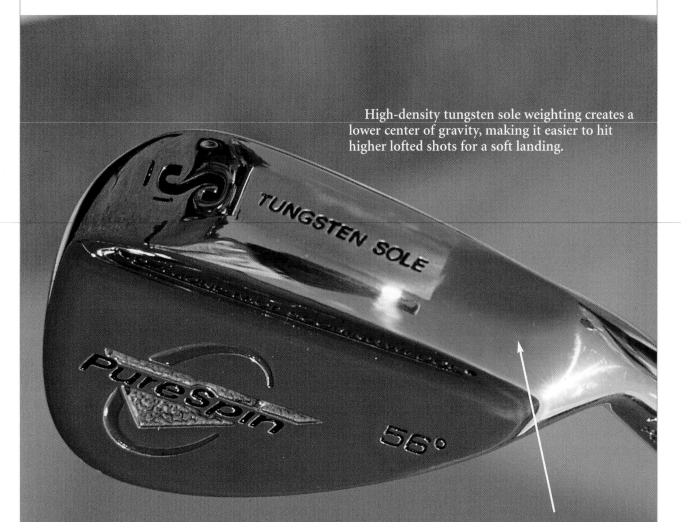

High-density tungsten sole weighting creates a lower center of gravity, making it easier to hit higher lofted shots for a soft landing.

Developed with feedback from the SENIOR PGA TOUR, this wedge features an improved rounded toe and leading edge.

This wedge features a four-way cambered sole, which minimizes ground resistance. For years, skilled players had to grind the bottom of their wedges to achieve this, something you can have done by looking for a clubfitter in your area. But now you can purchase the club ready to go to work.

CONSIDER CARRYING THREE WEDGES

Most TOUR players carry three wedges. At their skill level, being able to select the exact club needed for the shot at hand is vital.

Some companies now offer four wedges. The 52-degree wedge with eight degrees of bounce is sometimes referred to as an Attack or A-wedge.

PITCHING WEDGE OR GAP WEDGE

A pitching wedge or gap wedge offers 48 degrees of loft and 8 degrees of bounce, on average.

SAND WEDGE

A sand wedge provides 56 degrees of loft and 12 degrees of bounce, on average. Don't let the name fool you. A sand wedge is also effective from the fairway and rough, as well as bunkers.

LOB WEDGE

A lob wedge has the most loft—60 degrees on average, but some are 62 degrees. There are 3 degrees of bounce.

Scoring
Zone
Equipment

GLOSSARY

Address Your body position (posture, alignment, ball position) as you set up to the ball.

Addressing the Ball Taking a stance and grounding the club (except in a hazard) before taking a swing.

Approach A shot hit to the green.

Away A player who is farthest from the hole. This player plays his or her ball first.

Apron Slightly higher grassy area surrounding the putting surface. Also referred to as fringe.

Backspin The spin of a golf ball that is the opposite direction of the ball's flight.

Ball Mark The damaged, indented area in the ground caused by the ball when it lands on the green.

Ball Marker Something small to mark the position of your ball on the putting green. You should mark your ball to clean it and also allow your playing partners to have an unobstructed line to the hole. Markers can be purchased, and can be attached to your glove, or use a coin or similar object.

Birdie One stroke under the designated par of the hole.

Bogey One stroke over the designated par of the hole.

Bunker Also referred to as a sand trap.

Blade To hit the ball at its center with the bottom edge of your club.

Blocked Shot Hitting a ball on a straight line to the right.

Bump and Run A type of approach shot that lands and then rolls onto the green and toward the hole.

Carry How far a ball flies in the air. If a water hazard is in front of you, you have to figure the carry to be sure you've taken enough club.

Casual Water A temporary water accumulation not intended as a hazard. Consult the published *Rules of Golf* for information on the relief you are entitled to.

Chili-Dip Hitting the ground before contacting the ball. The result: weak, popped-up shots also called "fat."

Divot Turf displaced by a player's club when making a swing. Divots must be repaired.

Double Bogey Two strokes over the designated par for a hole.

Draw A shot that curves from right to left for right-handers and the opposite for left-handed golfers.

Drop The act of returning a ball back into play. Consult *The Rules of Golf* for correct information on circumstances where this occurs.

Eagle Two strokes under the designated par for a hole.

Fade A controlled, slight left-to-right ball flight pattern. Also can be called a cut.

Fairway Closely mowed route of play between tee and green.

Fore A warning cry to any person in the way of play or who may be within the flight of your ball.

Green The putting surface.

Gross Score Total number of strokes taken to complete a designated round.

Ground the Club Touching the surface of the ground with the sole of the club at address.

Handicap A deduction from a player's gross score. Handicaps for players are determined by guidelines published by the USGA.

Halved the Hole The phrase used to describe a hole where identical scores were made.

Honor The right to tee off first, earned by scoring the lowest on the previous hole.

Hook A stroke made by a right-handed player that curves the ball to the left of the target. It's just the opposite for left-handers.

Hosel The metal part of the clubhead where the shaft is connected.

Hot A ball that comes off the clubface without backspin and will go farther than normal as a result. If a lie puts grass between the clubface and ball, the grooves can't grip the ball to develop backspin. Understanding this, a golfer knows their ball will come out "hot" and plans for that.

Lateral Hazard A hazard (usually water) that is on the side of a fairway or green. Red stakes are used to mark lateral hazards.

Lie Stationary position of the ball. Also it is described as the angle of the shaft in relation to the ground when the club sole rests naturally.

Local Rules Special rules for the course that you are playing.

Loft The amount of angle built into the clubface.

Match Play A format where each hole is a separate contest. The winner is the individual or team that wins more holes than are left to play.

Mulligan A second ball that's hit from the same location. The shot that's tried again. Limited to friendly, noncompetitive rounds.

Net Score Gross score less handicap.

Par The score a golfer should make on a given hole. Determined by factoring in 2 putts plus the number of strokes needed to cover the yardage between the tee and green.

Provisional Ball A second ball hit before a player looks for his or her first ball, which may be out of bounds or lost.

Pull Shot A straight shot in which the flight of the ball is for right-handers and right of the target for left-handers.

Push Shot A straight shot in which the flight of the ball is right of the target for a right-handed golfer and left of the target for a left-hander.

Rough Areas of longer grass adjacent to the tee, fairway green or hazards.

Shank To hit a shot off the club's hosel.

Slice A stoke made across the ball, creating spin that curves the ball to the right of the intended target for right-handed golfers and to the left of the target for left-handers.

Stance Position of the feet at address.

Stroke Any forward motion of the clubhead made with an intent to strike the ball. The number of strokes taken on each hole are entered for that hole's score.

Stroke Play Competition based on the total number of strokes taken.

Target The spot or area a golfer chooses for the ball to land or roll.

Top To hit the ball above its center.

INDEX